VISITORS

★★★★★ "Remember the name Barney Norris. He's outstanding." *The Times*

★★★★★ "Barney Norris's astonishingly accomplished debut" *Evening Standard*

★★★★ "Infinitely touching. The real pleasure lies in discovering an authentic new voice." *Guardian*

★★★★ "An absolute beauty. Exceptional" *Daily Telegraph*

★★★★ "An excellent play, a sweet, subtle, sad tale." *Time Out Critics Choice*

★★★★ "Assured and affecting, a writer to watch" *Whatsonstage.com*

★★★★★ "This is an exceptionally good play. Linda Bassett triumphs." *Stage Talk*

★★★★★ "Masterful" *Auditorium*

★★★★ "A beautiful love story, a fantastic cast." *Islington Gazette*

★★★★ "Sharply funny, tender and at moments utterly eviscerating." *Exeunt*

★★★★ "Exquisite. Surely a future classic." *Fourth Wall*

Barney Norris

VISITORS

OBERON BOOKS
LONDON

WWW.OBERONBOOKS.COM

First published in 2014 by Oberon Books Ltd
521 Caledonian Road, London N7 9RH
Tel: +44 (0) 20 7607 3637 / Fax: +44 (0) 20 7607 3629
e-mail: info@oberonbooks.com
www.oberonbooks.com

A catalogue record for this book is available from the British
Library.

PB ISBN: 978-1-78319-104-8
E ISBN: 978-1-78319-603-6

Cover design by Matthew Ward

Printed and bound by Marston Book Services, Didcot.

For my grandparents, Albert and Margaret Norris.

With thanks to Frank and Elizabeth Brenan; Arts Council England, Christopher Benjamin, Lily Bevan, Anna Carr, Simon Chandler, Elizabeth Crarer, Mackenzie Crook, Matthew Deveraux, Rob Heaps, Janet Henfry, Roanna Lewis, Ralf Little, Pauline Munro, Owen Oakeshott, Craig Phelps, Lucie Regan, Eva Tausig and all the participants in the Salisbury workshop; John Burgess, Graham Cowley, Mehmet Ergen, Peter Gill, Josie Rourke, Patrick Sandford and Max Stafford-Clark for notes and notions for rejection; Annie Reilly and all at Nuffield Theatre Southampton; Gareth Machin, Mark Powell, Eugenia Whitby and all at Salisbury Playhouse; the Peggy Ramsay Foundation; Leo Butler and the Royal Court Young Writers Group; George Spender and Oberon Books; Rozzy Wyatt at Judy Daish Associates; the Arcola Theatre; the Bush Theatre; Jane Cotton and the Alzheimer's Society, Sue, David and Alzheimer's Research UK, the Carers Trust, Viola Brisolin and the Workers Educational Association, Beryl Mellish and the U3A; Judith Dimant and Lucy Williams at Complicite, Mark Douet, the Donmar Warehouse, Middlesex University, Hilary at the National Theatre, Out of Joint, RADA, Kate Morley PR, the Cornershop, Clean Break, London Bubble, Cressida Klaces, Sophie, Jeremy and Mahamed at Electronic Theatre Controls, and special thanks to Icarus Theatre for the loan of their van; Linda Bassett, George Dennis, Anouska Lester, Frank Moon, Francesca Reidy, Jasmine Sandalli, Robin Soans, Simon Gethin Thomas, Ally Watson and Eleanor Wyld, the most extraordinary company; and to Alice, Ashleigh, Charlie, Chloe, Jake, Matt and everyone else who has made Up In Arms.

Man is in love and loves what vanishes,
What more is there to say?

W.B. Yeats, *Nineteen Hundred and Nineteen*

UP IN ARMS

Honest, human, affecting, revealing:
we make plays about people and the places they're from.

Artistic Directors Alice Hamilton and Barney Norris
Producer Chloe Courtney
Associate Producer Ashleigh Wheeler
Company Stage Manager Charlie Young

Our work is built around a permanent ensemble of like-minded theatremakers. Our plays grow out of workshops and conversations over years, and through our Participation programme we work with hundreds of people each year, encouraging them to engage creatively with their lives through making theatre.

KEEP IN TOUCH – JOIN OUR MAILING LIST

www.upinarms.org.uk | director@upinarms.org.uk
Twitter: @upinarmstheatre | Facebook: "Up In Arms"

Supported using public funding by
LOTTERY FUNDED | ARTS COUNCIL ENGLAND

BUSH THEATRE

We make theatre for London. Now.

The Bush is a **world-famous** home for new plays and an internationally renowned champion of plays. We **discover, nurture and produce** the best new playwrights from the widest range of backgrounds from our home in a distinctive corner of west London.

The Bush has won over **100 awards** and developed an enviable reputation for touring its acclaimed productions nationally and internationally.

We are excited by exceptional new voices, stories and perspectives – particularly those with **contemporary bite** which reflect the **vibrancy of British culture** now.

Now located in a recently renovated library building on the Uxbridge Road in the heart of Shepherd's Bush, the theatre houses a 144-seat auditorium, rehearsal rooms and a lively café bar.

Supported by
ARTS COUNCIL ENGLAND

h&f
hammersmith & fulham

bushtheatre.co.uk

'A powerhouse of new writing'

Sunday Times Culture

Supporters

Our audiences make us who we are. We would like to thank the members of our Supporters Scheme, whose engagement with our work strengthens and nourishes it in dozens of different, vital ways.

To join the Up In Arms Supporters Scheme, access exclusive opportunities and become part of our work, visit **upinarms.org.uk.**

VERY SPECIAL THANKS

Frank and Elizabeth Brenan, Peter and Jane Hamilton, Alison Lowdon, Sarah Burslem, Pete and Ruth Shepherd

SPECIAL THANKS

Lauren Trimble and Offline Magazine, Susanna Bishop, Farhana Bhula, Bekah Diamond, Hasan Dixon, Esther Ruth Elliott, Victoria Gee, Juliette Kelly-Fleming, Max Lindsay, Alice Malin, Suzy McClintock, Linda Morse, Janet Rieder, George Warren

THANKS

Viola Brisolin and the Workers Educational Association, Lindsay Balkwell, Sarah Blake, Milly Ellis, Hannah Groombridge, Aidan Grounds, Luke Holbrook, Katharine Ingle, Naomi Petersen, Kandy Rohmann, Ivan Richardson, Frances Macadam

Company Biographies

Linda Bassett | Edie
Theatre includes: *Roots, Phaedra* (Donmar Warehouse); *People, Schism in England, Juno and the Paycock, A Place With The Pigs* (National) *Love & Information, In Basildon, Wastwater, The Stone, Lucky Dog, Far Away, East Is East, The Recruiting Officer, Our Country's Good, Serious Money, Aunt Dan and Lemon, Abel's Sister, Fen* (Royal Court); *A Winter's Tale, Pericles* (RSC); *The Road To Mecca* (Arcola); *Hortensia and the Museum of Dreams* (Finborough Theatre); *Love Me Tonight, The Awakening, Out In The Open* (Hampstead Theatre); *Richard III, The Taming Of The Shrew* (Globe); *John Gabriel Borkman* (ETC); *Five Kinds of Silence* (Lyric Hammersmith); *The Dove* (Croydon Warehouse); *The Triumph of Love* (Almeida); *The Clearing* (Bush Theatre); *The Seagull* (Liverpool Playhouse); *George Dandin, Medea, Woyceck, The Bald Prima Donna* (Leicester Haymarket/Liverpool Playhouse/Almeida); *The Cherry Orchard* (Leicester Haymarket); *Falkland Sound* (Belgrade Theatre Studio); Belgrade T.I.E Company (Coventry); Interplay Theatre Company (Leeds).
Film includes: *Effie, West Is West* (BBC Films); *Cass, The Reader, Kinky Boots, Separate Lies, Spivs, Calendar Girls, The Last Time, The Hours, The Martins, East Is East, Beautiful People, Oscar and Lucinda, Mary Reilly, Waiting for the Moon, Indian Summer.*
Television includes: *Call the Midwife, The Spies of Warsaw, The Life and Adventures of Nick Nickelby, Grandma's House* (2 series), *Larkrise To Candleford* (4 series), *Sense and Sensibility, This Little Life, Our Mutual Friend, Far From The Madding Crowd, Silent Film, Kavanagh Q.C., Casualty, Christmas, A Touch of Frost, Dinner Ladies, Love Hurts, A Small Dance, No Bananas, Eastenders, Say Hello To The Real Dr Snide, The Bill, Newshounds, A Village Affair, Bramwell, Loved Up, Cold Light Of Day, Frank Stubbs Promotes, Skallagrig.*
Radio includes: *Roots, Notes To Self, The Memory of Water, Freefall, Abishag The Virgin.*

Chloe Courtney | Producer
Chloe is currently Project Co-ordinator at Complicite and has been Up In Arms' Producer since 2012. She also works as an independent Producer and Development Manager for companies including Antler and Mouths of Lions, and has previously produced work for Oxford Playhouse, Wilderness Festival, Secret Garden Party, LIFT, Shunt Vaults and Liverpool's City of Culture celebrations.

Rebecca Denby | Assistant Stage Manager
Becky recently graduated from the University of Winchester.

George Dennis | Sound Designer
Theatre includes: *Beautiful Thing* (West End/UK Tour); *The Edge of Our Bodies, Dances of Death* (Gate Theatre); *Regeneration* (Royal & Derngate, UK Tour); *Mametz* (National Theatre of Wales); *Peddling* (also 59E59, New York) and *Moth* (also Bush Theatre) (HighTide Festival); *Minotaur* (Polka Theatre/Clwyd Theatr Cymru); *Spring Awakening* (Headlong); *The Island* (Young Vic); *Love Your Soldiers* (Sheffield Crucible Studio); *The Last Yankee* (Print Room); *Thark* (Park Theatre); *Hello/Goodbye* (Hampstead Theatre Downstairs); *Liar Liar* (Unicorn Theatre); *Good Grief* (Theatre Royal Bath/UK Tour); *The Seven Year Itch* (Salisbury Playhouse); *When Did You Last See My Mother?* (Trafalgar Studios 2); *The Seagull, The Only True History of Lizzie Finn* (Southwark Playhouse); *A Life, Foxfinder* (Finborough Theatre); *The Living Room* (Jermyn Street Theatre).

Alice Hamilton | Director
Theatre productions for Up In Arms include: *Visitors* (tour, Bush Theatre and Arcola Theatre, nominated for Best Director, Offies 2014), *Fear Of Music* (tour with Out of Joint) and *At First Sight* (tour and Latitude Festival). **Other theatre as Director includes:** *Extinct* and *Starcrossed* (Bush Theatre for Courting Drama), *Belarus* (Arcola Theatre for The Miniaturists) and *The Kingdom of Me* (Park Theatre for Hatch). She was recently assistant director on *Regeneration* (Northampton Royal and Derngate and tour) and *A Day in the Death of Joe Egg* (Liverpool Playhouse, Rose Theatre Kingston and tour). Forthcoming engagements include staff director on *Man And Superman* (National Theatre).

Anouska Lester | Costume Supervisor
Credits as designer include: *A Dream Play* and *A Little Night Music* (Oxford Playhouse); credits as costume supervisor include *Much Ado About Nothing* (Neuss Shakespeare Festival), *The Magic Toyshop, The Royal Hunt of the Sun, The Seagull* and *Arcadia* (Oxford Playhouse). Other credits include Wardrobe Assistant at the London Academy of Music and Dramatic Art and Costume Assistant on *Dead on Her Feet* (The North Wall).

Simon Muller | Stephen
Simon studied at Edinburgh University and trained at LAMDA.
Theatre includes: *Epsom Downs* (Salisbury Playhouse), *Government Inspector* (Young Vic), *The Odyssey, Hamlet, The Seagull* (The Factory), *Vanity Fair, The Winter's Tale* (Royal Lyceum, Edinburgh), *Love's Labour's Lost, In Extremis, Antony and Cleopatra, Romeo and Juliet* (Shakespeare's Globe), *The Grizzled Skipper, The Cage* (Nuffield, Southampton), *Venezuela* (Arcola), *Hamlet* (Haymarket, Basingstoke), *Markings* (Traverse Theatre and Southwark Playhouse), *War Stories* (AZ Theatre/OH!Art), *Habitats* (The Gate), *Natural Inclinations* (The Finborough), *The Lie* (King's Head), *As You*

Like It (Natural Perspectives).
Film includes: *Madam Bovary, Anna Karenina.*
Television includes: *Silent Witness, The Bill.*
Radio includes: *The Changeling* (BBC Radio 3).
Simon is an Associate Member of The Factory.

Barney Norris | Writer

This is Barney's first full-length play. His short plays *Fear Of Music,* toured in collaboration with Out of Joint, and his award-winning debut *At First Sight* have also been produced by Up In Arms. His book *To Bodies Gone: The Theatre of Peter Gill,* is published by Seren.

Francesca Reidy | Designer

Francesca is a graduate of RADA's postgraduate Theatre Design course. **Design credits include:** *The Railway Children* (FOH design, King's Cross Theatre), *Chef* (Underbelly, Edinburgh), *Housed* (Old Vic Theatre), *Venice Preserv'd* (Spectators Guild), *The Summer Book* (Unicorn), *BABY/LON* (Bighouse Theatre), *Amygdala* (Print Room), *Richard III* (East 15), *Godchild* (Hampstead), *Sunset Baby* (Gate), *Tommy* (Prince Edward Theatre), *The President and the Pakistani* (Waterloo East), *One Hour Only* (Old Vic New Voices Edinburgh), *Step 9 (Of 12)* (Trafalgar Studios), *Port Authority* (Southwark), *Phaedre* (Cockpit), *Arab Spring* (Arch 61), *The Shape of Things* (Gallery Soho), *Booty* (Only Connect), *Spring in June* (London Film Academy). She is the Associate Designer of Rhapsody of Words, The Helsingor Sewing Club and Troupe Theatre company. Francesca was one of the Jerwood Young Designers for 2012.

Josephine Rossen | Deputy Stage Manager

Josephine trained at Middlesex University.
Theatre includes: Stage Manager for *Free As Air* (Finborough), *The Seagull* (White Bear), *Le Nozze de Figaro, Carmen* (Winslow Hall Opera), *Clive and Other Stories* (Gestalt Arts); Deputy Stage Manager for *Broke* (Paper Birds, Greenwich); Assistant Stage Manager for *Fragile* (Cockpit Theatre).

Jasmine Sandalli | Production Manager

Jasmine graduated from Rose Bruford College with a BA Hons (First) in Stage Management in 2006.
Shows as Production Manager include: *This House,* 10 plays for *Connections 2013* (National Theatre); *Visitors* (UK tour and Arcola Theatre); *Little Women, A Man Of No Importance, A Catered Affair* and *Little Me* (Royal Academy of Music); *Cinderella* (Warwick Arts Centre); *The Hairy Ape* (Southwark Playhouse); *The Jitterbug Blitz, One Night Only, Contains Violence* and *The Luna Club* (Lyric Theatre Hammersmith).
Shows as Deputy Production Manager include: *One Man, Two*

Guvnors (National Theatre, Adelphi Theatre, UK Tour); *The Kitchen, Last of the Haussmans, Misterman, A Woman Killed With Kindness, Season's Greetings, Blood and Gifts, Hansel and Gretel, Holy Rosenbergs* (National Theatre); *Ghost Stories, Jack and the Beanstalk, Comedians, Punk Rock, Spring Awakening, Cinderella, Watership Down, Metamorphosis* (Lyric Theatre Hammersmith). Jasmine is currently Technical Operations Coordinator at the National Theatre, working on capital and infrastructure projects.

Robin Soans | Arthur
Theatre includes: *Hamlet, As You Like It, The Country Wife, Venetian Twins, Murder In The Cathedral* (RSC); *Someone Who'll Watch Over Me, The Belle's Stratagem* (Southwark Playhouse); *The Stock Da'Wa* (Hampstead Theatre); *Palace of The End, Pieces of Vincent* (Arcola Theatre); *The Rivals* (Southwark Playhouse); *Sixty-Six Books, On The Beach and Resilience, Raising Fires* (Bush Theatre); *Coriolanus* and *Under The Black Flag* (The Globe); *On Ego, Jump Mr Malinoff Jump* (Soho Theatre); *The Holy Terror* (Duke of Yorks West End); *Anything Goes* (National Theatre and Theatre Royal Drury Lane); *Loves Labours Lost, A Prayer For Owen Meany, The Invention of Love, The London Cuckolds, Volpone* (National Theatre); *Push Up, Waiting Room Germany, Three Birds Alighting On a Field, Etta Jenks, Star-Gazie Pie and Sauerkrout* (Royal Court); *Another Country* (Arts Theatre) *Ghosts* (Comedy Theatre) *Hamlet* (Plymouth/Young Vic), *Moonshine* (Plymouth/Hampstead), *Shopping and F***ing* (Royal Court/Out of Joint), *Fashion* (Leicester/Tricycle), *Bet Noir* (Young Vic), *Thatcher's Women* (Tricycle/UK tour).
Television includes: *Endeavour, Silk, Doctors, Casualty, Midsomer Murders, The Bill, Doctors, Waking The Dead, Holby City, Miss Marple, casualty, Dalziel & Pascoe, The Russian Bride, Dangerfield, Kavanagh, Far From The Madding Crowd, Jonathon Creek, Rebecca, Inspector Morse.*
Film includes: *The Last Hangman, The Queen, Not Only but Always, Method, The God Club, A.K.A, Sabotage.*
Plays include: *Perseverance Drive* (Bush Theatre), *Mixed Up North, Talking To Terrorists, A State Affair* (Out of Joint), *The Arab-Israeli Cookbook* (Gate Theatre).

Simon Gethin Thomas | Lighting Designer
Simon is a London-based Lighting Designer who trained for a Master's Degree at the Royal Welsh College of Music and Drama.
For Up In Arms: *Visitors* (Arcola and tour), *Fear Of Music* (tour with Out of Joint).
Previous credits include: *Eye of a Needle* (Southwark Playhouse), *Sweeney Todd* (Twickenham Theatre), *Pincher Martin* (Britten Theatre), *Othello: Deconstructed* (The North Wall, Oxford), *Gone Viral* , *I Cinna [The Poet]* (St James Theatre), *Girl From Nowhere* , *Woman in the Dunes* (Theatre 503) and for the *Arensky Chamber Orchestra* (Queen Elizabeth Hall, Southbank Centre).

Ally Watson | Assistant Director
Ally is a regular collaborator with award-winning companies Tap Tap Theatre and 1945 Productions.
Theatre as director includes: *Take It Interns* (Edinburgh Fringe), *Homecoming* (reading, Bristol Old Vic), *The Sky Tonight Is* (Lady Windsor Theatre), *Birds: A Triptych, Hornets* (Wardrobe Theatre).

Ashleigh Wheeler | Associate Producer
Ashleigh was recently Resident Producer at Oxford Playhouse, and has previously worked with the Invisible College and Out of Joint. She has most recently produced *Fiji Land* for Three Streets at the Southwark Playhouse.

Eleanor Wyld | Kate
Eleanor trained at the Guildhall School of Music and Drama.
Theatre includes: *Separate Tables, Bedroom Farce* (Salisbury Playhouse), *Unscorched, Rigor Mortis* (Finborough Theatre); *Dances of Death* (Gate Theatre); *The Astronaut's Chair* (Theatre Royal Plymouth); *Shiverman* (Theatre 503); *His Teeth* (Only Connect); *Antigone* (Southwark Playhouse); *The Deep Blue Sea* (West Yorkshire Playhouse); *Romeo and Juliet* (Brighton Dome/InService); *Liar* workshop (Bath Theatre Royal/National Theatre Young Company); *Amy's Wedding* (Youth Music Theatre: UK, The Garage Theatre, Norwich); *Nos Vie Un Rose* (NYMT, Birmingham Hippodrome).
Television includes: *Holby City* (BBC); *Doctors* (BBC); *Misfits* Series 4 (Channel 4); *Black Mirror: The National Anthem* (Channel 4); *Casualty* (BBC); *Honest* (Greenlit Productions); *You Can Choose Your Friends* (Avalon); *Coronation Street* - 2 Episodes (Granada).
Film includes: *Bonobo* (Bonobo Films); *Johnny English Reborn* (Intelligence Films Ltd); *The Manual* (Britpack Film Company); *Freestyle* (Revolver Films).

Charlie Young | Company Stage Manager
Charlie trained at Middlesex University.
For Up In Arms: *Visitors* (Arcola and tour), *Fear Of Music* (tour with Out of Joint).
Recent stage management credits include: *Emily Brown and the Thing* (Tall Stories), *Blind* (Paper Birds), *Barbican Box* (Barbican), *Between Us* (Arcola Theatre), *Idylls of the King* (Oxford Playhouse), *Amazon Beaming* workshop (Complicite), *Pinocchio* (Berry Theatre, Eastleigh), *Hag* and *The Girl With The Iron Claws* (The Wrong Crowd), *The Snail and the Whale* (Tall Stories), *Jesus Christ Superstar* (Ljubljana, Slovenia), *The Hairy Ape* (Southwark Playhouse) and *Third Floor* (Trafalgar Studios).
Forthcoming engagements include: *The Snail and the Whale* (Tall Stories).

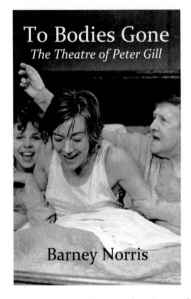

To Bodies Gone
The Theatre of Peter Gill

Barney Norris

To Bodies Gone is the first study of one of the most significant voices of modern international theatre. Written by an assistant and friend with an intimate, personal knowledge of Gill's processes and values, *To Bodies Gone* explores the eminent career of playwright and director Peter Gill.

Analysing the phases of his career, this study places Gill in the wider context of the theatre, providing a snapshot of theatre in the second half of the twentieth century and contributing new insights to the study of theatre history.

To Bodies Gone includes chapters on Gill's early work, influences (Lawrence, Chekhov, Beckett), his translations and adaptations (Lawrence, Chekhov, Wedekind, Faulkner), his directing career at the Royal Court, Riverside Studios, National Theatre and NT Studio, plus his major plays – *Small Change*, *Kick for Touch*, *In the Blue*, *Cardiff East*, *The York Realist* and his 2014 play, set at the Versailles peace conference. The result is a major study full of insight into Gill and into British Theatre.

Price £14.99

Pub date: 15 Feb 2014

available from www.serenbooks.com

Visitors was first performed at the Everyman Theatre, Cheltenham on 10 February 2014 with the following cast:

Linda Bassett – EDIE

Simon Muller – STEPHEN

Robin Soans – ARTHUR

Eleanor Wyld – KATE

Writer, Barney Norris

Director, Alice Hamilton

Designer, Francesca Reidy

Lighting Designer, Simon Gethin Thomas

Sound Designer, Frank Moon

Production Manager, Jasmine Sandalli

Stage Manager, Charlie Young

Costume Supervisor, Anouska Lester

Assistant Director, Ally Watson

Producer, Chloe Courtney

Participation Producer, Ashleigh Wheeler

The production transferred to the Bush Theatre and opened on 26 November 2014.

Linda Bassett – EDIE

Simon Muller – STEPHEN

Robin Soans – ARTHUR

Eleanor Wyld – KATE

Writer, Barney Norris

Director, Alice Hamilton

Designer, Francesca Reidy

Lighting Designer, Simon Gethin Thomas

Sound Designer, George Dennis

Production Manager, Jasmine Sandalli

Company Stage Manager, Charlie Young

Deputy Stage Manager, Josephine Rossen

Assistant Stage Manager, Rebecca Denby

Costume Supervisor, Anouska Lester

Producer, Chloe Courtney

Associate Producer, Ashleigh Wheeler

Characters

ARTHUR
about 70, a farmer

EDIE
about 70, a farmer's wife

STEPHEN
about 40, middle management in an insurance firm

KATE
20s, a university graduate

The play is set in the main room of a farm
in north Wiltshire.

Act One

The main room of a farmhouse in north Wiltshire. EDIE and ARTHUR are sitting in chairs.

EDIE: We were having coffee on the beach. From a flask. And I had the lid and you drank straight from the nozzle. We walked there didn't we, that's the only way to get over. Up early, breakfast in the hotel, then down to the cove and up again round the cliff path till you see the second beach stretching out under you. It was cold, with the wind off the sea. We were just about warm enough in the sun but when you went into the shade…the sun was on the shingle so we thought we'd sit down. And we saw the most beautiful thing. She was all in white.

ARTHUR: Edie –

EDIE: Not now Arthur. She was all in white and in a way it was very unflashy. A simple dress almost, sheer down her sides then trailing out behind her. High neck, low back. You can do that if you have the figure. I don't think I ever did. She had the blackest hair, and such a smile. White teeth. Dark skin. The groom was just a boy. He looked too young for her. I suppose they must have been the same age. She would have better suited an older man, someone with a bit of – something about him. But you could tell they were enjoying themselves.

ARTHUR: We had a lovely wedding.

EDIE: Oh…

ARTHUR: In the church. A beautiful day. You wouldn't think it, my luck, but the sun and the trees and the church yard, 'member? They'd mowed the grass. 'Member the smell of it. Lovely day, bright in the church with the light coming in through the windows. That was the happiest day of my

21

life. I remember you coming up the aisle, and your Dad, and my heart beating that hard. When I was young I used to worry about crying at the altar. When I was a boy and imagined it, I used to be really worried I'd burst into tears. But it wasn't like that. I felt proud, and so, excited. Felt like we were getting it done.

EDIE: Then we came here. It's always been so light in the kitchen and I used to sing while I made tea in the morning, do you remember how your father hated that? He was funny. Were our lives like everyone else's? The mornings always seem so light, though they're not as bright as the middle of the day. I love how sharp the line across the garden cuts the air when you catch a sight through the kitchen window. That's the best way to dry clothes. They can't improve everything. Back then our nearest neighbours were the Joneses and the Parks. I liked the Joneses, where did they go? They had those dogs. But they were nice people. Did they have enough or go bust, which was it?

ARTHUR: Didn' mind those dogs. Meant he couldn' sneak around.

EDIE: You always knew Ted Jones was going round his yard with the barking, yes. He didn't go mad? Am I remembering – ? It was yellow wallpaper when I first came here. I did feel grown up. That was the first time I felt grown up and it was exciting, because we weren't really, were we?

ARTHUR: I used to worry before we were married. Used to worry there was something wrong with me. 'Cause I had a beautiful girl, and some days, when I didn't see you, I didn't miss you. I was happy to just get on. I could not think about you all day. You were always so pleased to see me, I used to wonder, how can I only miss her some of the time? Then I'd miss you something terrible, wouldn' be able to sleep for thinking.

EDIE: It's all right. I was the same. I didn't think about you either. I used to worry about you was all. You out there in

the wheat fields and me in town with whatever errands. I
worried I might not get home in time to get your tea out.

ARTHUR: Edie –

EDIE: We mustn't make a thing of today. It'll be harder for her.

ARTHUR: This might be the last time we're ever alone like this.

EDIE: No it won't. I don't know what you think's happening
but it's not like that.

ARTHUR: It's just –

EDIE: She was all in white. He wasn't old enough, but they did
look lovely standing in their good shoes on the shingle.
There was a man in black with a camera buzzing round
them. You know how flies land on bright colours? You
know how cats sit on cushions? Wherever there's a cushion
in a room, a cat will sit on it. That's what beauty's like,
people want to be near it. The only thing that's beautiful
is youth. That's when you still have your life to live, that's
beautiful. That's what people are looking at when they
love something. Even you and me. What I'm seeing when
I look at you is the whole past, isn't it. Our lives curled
round each other like ferns half furled. They're deceptive,
photographs. Wedding snaps especially.

ARTHUR: Why?

EDIE: You look at a wedding photograph, it looks like the end
of a story. I spose that's the books we read when we're
babies. But it's not an ending, is it? It's not a start either.
Just another day really.

ARTHUR: Oh.

EDIE: No, I mean, of course it's special. You know I think that.
But it doesn't stop there, does it. Nothing's fixed. You have
to keep working.

ARTHUR: Oh, I see. Oh yes. You have to keep on.

EDIE: He should be here by now. Is that clock right?

ARTHUR: Wound it up this morning so we'd know when
they'd arrive.

EDIE: I wish she'd just come and we could get the first cup of tea out the way.

ARTHUR: Feels like an ending an all. Doesn't it come quick? Whoosh! Was that it? Yup, that was your life mate. How long do you think we've got?

EDIE: Oh, don't. I've got longer than you have.

ARTHUR: Oh, you –

EDIE: We used to laugh, didn't we? You used to say you'll never catch me up.

ARTHUR: You won't, you know. I've still got years on you. My young thing.

EDIE: If I could choose any life I don't think I'd have things very different from this. These chairs are very comfortable. Do you get tired sitting up? I've got you, and you make me laugh. Perhaps if I could have been a despot and lived without a thought for anyone else. What are their names, the very bad ones? It must have been blissful to be Pol Pot or Hitler, they could do what they wanted, they were mad, it didn't matter to them. They could have made the shops open later just like that. I suppose we're all mad aren't we, they just got to show it off. But I've enjoyed all this.

ARTHUR: I would have liked to have experienced the sixties.

EDIE: Well you were alive in them.

ARTHUR: I mean I would have liked to have tried LSD.

EDIE: We still could, you know, they still make it. Shall we get some? Would you have liked free love?

ARTHUR: I wouldn't have got any and you would have got loads.

EDIE: There won't be as much of that now we've got company.

ARTHUR: Ho ho.

EDIE: Do you miss that? Sexual love?

ARTHUR: Yes.

EDIE: Yes. We could try that. Nights when she's out. Bit of romantic lighting. How long did we plan for that holiday? Half my life it seems we talked. All I remember's you complaining about the price of parking.

ARTHUR: Oh my love, I'm sorry.

EDIE: I'm joking, aren't I.

ARTHUR: I've been selfish to you all my life.

EDIE: No you weren't, shut up.

ARTHUR: I was.

EDIE: Don't let's talk about big things now.

ARTHUR: When can I?

EDIE: I don't know. Not today.

ARTHUR: Look – I never could argue with you.

EDIE: You always tried. You'd get so cross because you never had an answer. You'd go out to the shed to sulk.

ARTHUR: I get a lot done in that shed.

EDIE: I know you did, love. You've always been good at mending.

ARTHUR: Anyone can fix anything with a bit of care, I wasn't special. Patient.

EDIE: You had a knack.

ARTHUR: Practice.

EDIE: Don't be modest. I've always been proud.

ARTHUR: Didn't you mind?

EDIE: What?

ARTHUR: That everything was mended. We didn't buy much new. I always fixed things, but I used to think maybe things broke for a reason. Maybe we'd rather a new thing. All those women, your friends, used to go on about their machines, their sofas. We never did. I fixed the old ones. Did you feel left out? Would you have preferred it if I'd

25

spent a bit more money? I don't want to have been tight. Did I come across as tight-fisted?

EDIE: Oh my love.

ARTHUR: Does that mean I was or I wasn't?

EDIE: Of course you weren't. Besides, we bought things. All the new electronics. When I wanted a dishwasher we got one, didn't we?

ARTHUR: But was the house dowdy, did you think that?

EDIE: You worry too much. I thought it looked like us. What'll happen after us, d'you think?

ARTHUR: Some stranger will live here.

EDIE: I suppose it's for the best.

ARTHUR: I used to hope the boy'd change his mind. But he's all set up, isn't he. We took too long.

EDIE: Don't talk soft. We'll take a while yet. We've ten years in us. Twenty.

ARTHUR: Christ, imagine that.

EDIE: You do make me laugh. My love. We could lay traps for whoever lives here after.

ARTHUR: What do you mean?

EDIE: False floorboards. Alarm clocks hidden in the walls. Make them believe in ghosts. Look at this.

She gets up, crosses the room, stands on a creaky board.

EDIE: We could make everything make noises like that. Would it be possible to rig a cupboard door in such a way that every time you opened it, something happened to the toaster? Could you do that?

ARTHUR: Maybe.

EDIE: Or a window swing open. Or every time the window swings open for the door to close. I'd love that.

She neatens the room.

ARTHUR: It was so quiet, wasn't it. You could have sat there all day, if you could only keep warm. And watch the light changing through Durdle Door as if you looked into another world. Sit and do nothing. It would be wonderful to live like that.

EDIE: If I could have just one day again with my old legs and my old vitality and know while I had it how precious it was. I wouldn't do anything special, you know I never liked cake or rollercoasters or anything, maybe the seaside, nothing particular. I just didn't know how fast it would all get behind me.

She sits down.

ARTHUR: Do you think a lot of people have heart attacks at Lulworth Cove? Walking up that chalk path over the hill? I should think it's a hazard of the landscape.

EDIE: It's all right Arthur. You don't have to be frightened. It's just us two talking together.

ARTHUR: Edie.

EDIE: Don't be scared.

ARTHUR: I think in a way it's better never to live by the sea at all than live by the sea and have to put up with a shingle beach.

EDIE: Do you think I could have got away with a dress like that?

ARTHUR: You would have put her to shame. My young thing.

A knock at the door.

ARTHUR: That'll be her. *(Shouts.)* It's open, come in! Hello? We won't get up, come in!

EDIE: Will that be Stephen?

ARTHUR: He wouldn't knock. He hasn't come in time. Hello?

EDIE: Arthur.

ARTHUR: Can you hear me? Open the door and come in!

EDIE: Arthur?

27

ARTHUR: Yes love?

EDIE: You were just right.

ARTHUR: You what love?

EDIE: Just right.

ARTHUR: Oh God.

He gets up.

ARTHUR: Come in!

KATE enters.

KATE: I hope you don't mind, I let myself / in.

ARTHUR: Oh dear.

ARTHUR falls.

KATE: Oh my / God. Are you all right?

EDIE: Arthur? Arthur?

ARTHUR: I'm all right.

KATE: Don't get up on your own.

EDIE: Arthur?

ARTHUR: Timbeeer!

KATE: Can you get up? All right? That's good.

EDIE: Arthur?

ARTHUR: I'm all right. Whoo!

KATE: Back in the chair.

ARTHUR: Yep. Yep.

EDIE: Arthur?

ARTHUR: Didn't you hear me? I was shouting.

KATE: I'm sorry, I couldn't –

ARTHUR: It's fine. Edie, are you all right?

KATE: Should I –

ARTHUR: Wait a second. Are you all right Edie?

EDIE: Just right.

ARTHUR: I'm sorry about that. You're Kate, then?

KATE: Yes. Listen I'm so / sorry –

ARTHUR: Edie, are you all right?

EDIE: Just tired.

ARTHUR: That's all right. I'm sorry. Right. Why don't you take a seat and we can all calm down?

KATE: OK.

ARTHUR: No, would you do something for me? Could you get us all a cup of tea? It's good for a scare.

KATE: OK.

ARTHUR: The kitchen's through there. She doesn't take sugar and I take four.

KATE: OK.

ARTHUR: There's not an electric kettle so you boil it on the AGA.

KATE: That's fine.

ARTHUR: Thank you. I'd like to make it for you but I feel shook up.

KATE: Do you want me to call a doctor? Are you sure you're all right?

ARTHUR: Just through there.

KATE: OK.

KATE goes into the kitchen. ARTHUR gets up and goes to EDIE.

ARTHUR: There you go. Did I scare you? I'm sorry. You know where you are?

EDIE: I'm all right. You gave me a fright.

ARTHUR: Imagine how I feel. I'm going to sit down.

EDIE: Do you mind if I just have a rest?

ARTHUR: Of course. You sit back. All right? All right.

ARTHUR straightens.

ARTHUR: Working all day but I can't get out of an armchair now?

EDIE: Comes and goes, doesn't it.

ARTHUR: Apparently so.

Enter KATE.

KATE: Oh Mr Wakeling, you're out of your chair.

ARTHUR: That's very astute of you, yes. I thought I would reassure you that I'm not in fact an infirm old bastard, by sitting down unaided. *(He does so.)* There. I'm sorry we've met in – inauspicious circumstances. We were having a good day till you got here. Not that you – I only mean, call me Arthur. We're Arthur and Edie, you don't have to call me Mr Wakeling. I had the misfortune to be born with a surname made me sound like a cake.

EDIE: I don't know what I was thinking when I married him. My name was Wardley, it was perfectly nice. I might have been a nice old maid with more time for my lacework.

KATE: The kettle's on. It's got one of those singing –

ARTHUR: Do you want to sit down till it does?

KATE: Yeah, sure.

ARTHUR: I'm sorry my son's not here, he wanted to be here before you. You've met before though?

KATE: Yes, he met me last week. I'm sorry I'm only meeting you now. There's normally a thing first, but I was away.

ARTHUR: No bother. We figured you're all signed up, someone must think you're all right. Steve said you were all right. I just hope you think we're all right, is all.

EDIE: Pair of wrung out funny old dishcloths is us.

ARTHUR: Yes. Well. We don't get a lot of visitors out here, it's a red letter – been fun planning. You know? Having to fit in with a – yes. Well. Where have you been then while you were away?

KATE: I was WWOOFING.

ARTHUR: You what?

KATE: It's an acronym for a travel thing. Working on organic farms. It's this network of farms that put you up all over Europe if you do a bit of work.

ARTHUR: I didn't know they were sending us a farmer.

KATE: Well –

ARTHUR: We're not an organic farm. Nothing bad, just pesticides an that for killing the insects.

EDIE: And the moles.

ARTHUR: And the moles of course, we do them with traps.

EDIE: Snap!

KATE: I was really happy when I found out where you lived.

ARTHUR: Did you grow up on a farm, or –

KATE: No, I'm new to it. But I loved it.

ARTHUR: See if you're saying that after fifty years.

EDIE: Oh –

KATE: Have you always farmed?

ARTHUR: I've been here all my life.

KATE: In this house?

ARTHUR: Family farm. My father and his father before him.

KATE: That's amazing.

ARTHUR: Well. Where were you when you were farming?

KATE: I went round France. Lots of time around Clermont-Ferrand.

ARTHUR: I don't know France.

KATE: It's nice. It's better coming back to England.

ARTHUR: Oh yes. Will you go again next year?

KATE: I don't think so. It's tiring, isn't it, fields.

ARTHUR: I can't help but notice that you have blue hair.

EDIE: I had both hands wrapped round this thermos flask lid that stayed absolutely cool even though the drink in it was hot, and the steam from the coffee rising up. You're only really meant to drink it in the morning. And we saw this woman who was so very beautiful. She was getting married on the beach, they must have had a special licence. They were playing the Beach Boys on a portable cassette player. *(She sings 'God Only Knows', wordlessly.)*

ARTHUR: I should say now, Edie's not always able to keep up with a conversation. That's one of the things, why Steve's got you in.

EDIE: When we were first married I thought we'd have so many children, boys and girls. I think it's a shame there was only Stephen in the end.

ARTHUR: She remembers some things very clearly. Other things she finds hard.

KATE: I see.

ARTHUR: It's not something to be scared around. The thing to do is talk to her.

EDIE: I feel tired, Arthur.

ARTHUR: I know love, we'll get you upstairs soon. When her mother was dying she was the same. Not that Edie's – it's just similar, you know. But her mother was getting worse and worse, except when Edie used to read her a book. In between books her mind was unspooling, but when there was something to hold her attention –

KATE: I know the thing you mean, yeah.

EDIE: And it's very sad but we learn to get on with it.

ARTHUR: We were happy when Steve read about your thing on the internet, it'll make everything nicer having someone here.

EDIE: We have been to France, Arthur.

ARTHUR: I know. But the north, not to Clermont –

KATE: Ferrand.

EDIE: It was only a channel hop. But when I was forty we went to France. On the ferry.

KATE: Oh yeah?

EDIE: Have you ever heard of a catamaran?

KATE: Yeah, I have, yeah.

EDIE: Do they still have them?

KATE: I think so. I've never been on one.

EDIE: Oh, holidays are wonderful, you should go on as many holidays as you can. They float on top of the water.

ARTHUR: Catamarans.

EDIE: Shut up, she knows. They float on the water like skimming a stone. But you can take your car and everything.

KATE: Oh yeah?

EDIE: I don't know why he's acting superior. He was sick into the wind and it went all over him.

ARTHUR: I wasn't very good at the catamaran.

EDIE: Arthur doesn't like a journey, he likes to stay at home. I like looking forward to something.

ARTHUR: I have to stay at home, I've got a farm to run.

KATE: Holidays, you mean?

EDIE: Well, anything really. I don't think there'll be a lot more holidays for me.

KATE: You never know.

EDIE: I can be relatively confident. When you were a child where did you go when you went away?

KATE: Oh, loads of places I guess.

EDIE: You didn't have one house you'd always go to?

KATE: We used to go a lot to the same bit of Devon. Not really the same house.

ARTHUR: More of a caravan girl?

EDIE: Arthur! He thinks caravans are for the working class.

ARTHUR: How can I, I am working class, I work all the time.

EDIE: Yes, but we own all our furniture.

KATE: We did do a bit of caravanning.

EDIE: Oh yes?

KATE: It was – pretty chavvy, yeah. But you don't notice at the time, do you.

EDIE: I suppose they're comfortable inside. And what did you do before you were in France?

KATE: I was at uni. In Scotland.

EDIE: Oh yes? And what did you study?

KATE: Law.

EDIE: Really?

KATE: Yeah. It was good. It's hard to get work, but. I mean I don't know how I'll ever do anything with it. It was a good time though.

EDIE: And what is it you want to do then? After you're done with this kind of thing?

KATE: You mean –

EDIE: If you're looking after farms one year and the elderly the next, and you won't be a lawyer, what's it all with a view to?

The kettle starts to sing.

KATE: That's the kettle. I'd better get the tea.

ARTHUR: Thank you.

KATE: I won't be a moment.

EDIE: All right love.

KATE exits.

ARTHUR: Be nice to her, all right?

EDIE: What did I say?

ARTHUR: She probably doesn't know what she wants to do.

EDIE: Maybe she wants to do this.

ARTHUR: Hardly anyone thinks they're doing what they want to, do they?

EDIE: That's the saddest thing about you that you think that.

Enter KATE.

KATE: One with none one with four.

EDIE: Arthur.

ARTHUR: Well –

KATE: He won't have it every time.

ARTHUR: I am here, you know.

EDIE: You won't be for long if you put that much sugar in your tea.

ARTHUR: All right, all right. So tell us, Kate. What does your father do?

KATE: Well my Mum's a dinner lady.

ARTHUR: In a school?

KATE: Yeah, a primary school. I'm not in touch with my Dad.

ARTHUR: Me and Steve have been a bit hit and miss over the years.

KATE: Actually I've never known my Dad. We don't know who he is.

ARTHUR: Where is Steve anyway? He was supposed to get here before you.

KATE: It was really kind of him to meet me last week.

ARTHUR: Kind doesn't come into it, he wanted the day away.

EDIE: Arthur.

ARTHUR: His interest is himself, he doesn't really care for other people. He'd put you away if he could afford it.

EDIE: Arthur!

ARTHUR: Thing is, he can't. There's no money to show for all the work we've done. Steve moved away to make more of himself, but he hasn't really. I'm not trying to be cruel. I just mean he hasn't made much more money than he might have if he'd stayed with us. Life insurance. Seems a stupid business. You always pay out, don't you? Everyone always dies.

EDIE: That's not kind Arthur. He's a wonderful boy. And some people don't get their payouts if their policies lapse. Didn't you think he was a wonderful boy?

KATE: Well –

EDIE: He's always been good hearted. But didn't you like him? He's hard to get on with, but you liked him, didn't you?

KATE: Yeah –

ARTHUR: I've been cruel, haven't I? I'm sorry, I'd planned this conversation so you'd think we were all right but it's not going quite how I wanted.

EDIE: That's what happens to me.

KATE: Oh yes?

EDIE: Imagine I was a gardener. And I'd decided to pack all the gardening in. I don't know, maybe I couldn't be bothered. Maybe my back was gone. Well some of the paths get overgrown, so I can't walk down them. But some are still open, so I walk down them instead. And they're so unfamiliar, I haven't been down them in years. I'll try to tell Arthur about my day and all I can think is the way he threw up on the catamaran and I ended up sponging him clean, as if he were dough I were kneading. You know?

KATE: Right.

EDIE: I don't think you do. It's hard to explain. What you want to say builds up like water behind a dam but the dam will never open again. You talk about the past when you mean to ask for the butter knife. Or when you talk about little things what you think of is the things you love, and you want to talk about them, but the words won't come. And they will never come again. The best thing about having you here will be help in the kitchen.

KATE: Yes?

EDIE: I don't trust myself any more with the electric bread knife, and sometimes when I'm draining the potatoes, I say to myself do you know what, this is too heavy for you, you're going to drop this. I find if you say that it tends to buy you a bit of time.

KATE: Well I can help in the kitchen.

EDIE: We don't need help in the bathroom.

ARTHUR: Unless we get stuck in the bath.

EDIE: I have a way of getting up the stairs that's about swinging myself up on my arms, and it looks a bit dangerous, but you mustn't worry. Sometimes if I'm tired I find it easier to go down the stairs one by one on my backside, but you mustn't worry about that either. I think everyone would go down stairs like that if they didn't think it looked funny.

KATE: Right.

EDIE: We get up very early and go to bed early because we don't sleep well. Things have to have a routine because that's going to be good for me as I get worse. We sleep in different rooms because we keep each other up. Most days we're not as odd as you've found us, today is a red letter day because you're arriving and it's a bit more excitement than we're used to so we're talking too much.

ARTHUR: We'll talk less once we've calmed down.

KATE: You're not talking too much.

ARTHUR: I suppose it feels a lot because we hardly talk at all on an ordinary day. I think we're both worried you've changed your mind and you're thinking of leaving.

KATE: I'm not. I'm excited to be here.

ARTHUR: How long are you planning to stay?

EDIE: Oh, Arthur –

KATE: No, it's important you have some idea. So – honestly – well you asked me what I wanted to do. And the thing is, I'm not quite sure at the moment. Cos the thing with me, the thing is I'm just a bit mad. I finished school, and went to uni, and that was all great, but now there isn't really anything for me, and there's nothing I want to – go after, either. So I went round France because I wanted to take some time out and it sounded like fun, but you can't actually take time out of your life, can you, you're just losing time. So I'd signed up for this programme before I left, this homeshare thing, so for as long as I don't know what I want to do eventually, I'm happy to be here. Because it feels like I'm helpful. So I was thinking I'd stay for a while?

ARTHUR: It's been such a change in our lifetime, how people fix up their lives. For me and Edie, I don't think it entered our heads we'd do anything very different to this. It's what we were born to, isn't it. Then for Steve when he left, my son decided he didn't want to farm you see, you've met him haven't you, and that was a big choice, that was deciding to break with something. That was a big fight we had then. But in the end we thought, that's probably what progress looks like, because he can have a better life now. And perhaps he has. Now to hear you talk it's like it's changed again.

KATE: How?

ARTHUR: There's no question you might do anything other than go off looking for a life for yourself. That you might inherit anything.

KATE: I suppose not.

ARTHUR: I don't mean things, I mean your life.

KATE: I know what you mean.

ARTHUR: I suppose you're much freer.

KATE: Maybe, yeah.

EDIE: Opportunity. Much more is possible, it's wonderful really.

KATE: Yes.

ARTHUR: I wonder what you lose. Do you think you have to fight for things, do you think that still happens?

KATE: I don't know. I find everything difficult, but that might just be me.

ARTHUR: Causes, that's what used to be possible to come by. The Worker's Alliance Party. People used to aspire to things. Does that still happen?

KATE: Sort of. There's a lot of aspiring. I don't know what to.

ARTHUR: I suppose that's what happens when everyone finally gets a bit of money. After the war –

EDIE: Oh –

ARTHUR: There was nothing, you had to really want a thing to get it. You wouldn't believe it now. There was nothing, there was nothing, there was no string, nothing. We used to save paper bags on a nail over that fireplace. You can't describe it. I was hardly born. But I remember.

EDIE: She was all in white, and in a way it was very unflashy. A sheer dress, almost, straight down her body then flowing out like champagne overflowing the banks of a glass.

The clock strikes four.

ARTHUR: How is your tea?

KATE: Fine thanks.

ARTHUR: Steve was meant to be here an hour ago.

KATE: Probably traffic.

ARTHUR: Over Salisbury Plain? When he got here I was planning to properly settle you in. Show you the house and where you'd be sleeping. He's ruined it now, I feel like you've come in all backwards.

KATE: It's fine, really.

ARTHUR: I should have made the tea as well, I'm sorry, I wanted to check Edie. But she was all right and I should have made the tea.

EDIE: Of course I was.

ARTHUR: You're not always.

KATE: Mr Wakeling, it's fine. Don't worry. I know it's a bit weird me coming here. It's a bit weird for me too. It's all right if it's awkward.

ARTHUR: I thought we could all have dinner together, the four of us later.

KATE: That'd be lovely.

ARTHUR: You don't have to eat with us every day. We want you to treat this place as your own, and live how you want as much as possible. It's only if we need you we'll ask for anything.

KATE: Thank you.

ARTHUR: Will you be all right?

KATE: What do you mean?

ARTHUR: Well what worries us is we're out in the middle of nowhere. Will you be all right living here? There's not much in the way of fun.

KATE: This is what I'm looking for. A bit of quiet.

EDIE: It's the wrong time in your life to be looking for that.

KATE: Maybe.

ARTHUR: You have to tell us if you start to go mad, because we don't want to be trouble. Steve gave me the papers about this programme you're on, it seemed to me most of the kids who did it went to cities, part of the attraction was finding somewhere cheap to live in London or – Manchester. Did you not want that?

EDIE: We didn't think we'd find anyone, you know.

KATE: No?

EDIE: We advertised and you were the only person who replied.

ARTHUR: You're not on the run or anything, are you?

KATE: What from?

EDIE: He's joking. You're not in hiding from the police or something stupid?

KATE: Oh, no. Nothing like that.

EDIE: That's all right then.

ARTHUR: Not that we thought you might be. It was just a little joke we had. I feel like this has all gone wrong.

KATE: Really, it hasn't. It's great.

EDIE: You make a good cup of tea.

KATE: I'm glad.

ARTHUR: Well I'm glad we've got all that sorted out. It's important to arrange things, isn't it. I'm glad we've had this chat.

EDIE: When I was a young woman and hadn't met Arthur I used to imagine my husband. Did you used to do that?

KATE: All the time, yeah.

EDIE: How did you see him?

KATE: I don't know really. I thought he'd be tall. Mysterious, maybe.

EDIE: Then when you got older you got interested in other things about him.

KATE: Yeah, I guess so. By then I was trying them out though.

EDIE: Husbands?

KATE: Boys, yeah.

EDIE: I never had a chance for that.

KATE: No?

ARTHUR: Get in early, that was my plan.

EDIE: Oh –

ARTHUR: We met very young.

KATE: How old?

EDIE: I was eleven and he was thirteen.

KATE: Cheeky.

EDIE: Nothing happened for a long time.

ARTHUR: A very long time.

EDIE: My Dad was the groundsman of the golf course, and Arthur was poaching in the wood at the edge. So one day I was walking in the woods with my friend, and we caught him passing the other way with a trout under his arm.

ARTHUR: Ticklin' em up.

EDIE: I knew what he was doing, and I said excuse me, this is my father's golf course, what do you think you're doing walking over it? And he said –

ARTHUR: I'm the postman!

EDIE: Then he ran off.

KATE: Cheeky!

ARTHUR: Good fish that.

KATE: Did you have your eye on her from then, then?

ARTHUR: Oh yeah. Only took, what, seven more years after that?

EDIE: I never told on him so I think I must have liked him even then. He was an idiot at school.

ARTHUR: I never tried at school, I knew what I was doing after.

EDIE: I remember being like you though.

KATE: Like me?

EDIE: At the start of everything. And you're unsure because you could be anyone, really, and you don't know which life to have. When you're our age you feel unsure because you don't know whether you did it as well as you could have.

ARTHUR: And you haven't really.

EDIE: There are days and days you can't remember, after all. But the worst is in between you and me, to be Stephen, in your life, set on your course, and just not sure whether you're doing it right.

STEPHEN: *(Off.)* Hello!

ARTHUR: That's Steve. You won't say I fell, will you?

KATE: Really?

ARTHUR: Please don't.

KATE: I can't –

Enter STEPHEN.

STEPHEN: Sorry I'm late.

SCENE TWO

EDIE: What was – I'm in the park and he's coming to give me my birthday present. We're meeting on my lunch, I'm still at school and he's left, you see. What was – I sit on a bench near the school entrance to the park, just the other side of this hedge from the main gate, that's where everyone goes to have a cigarette. But I wasn't there for a fag. Why had I – ? Oh yes. He comes in the park and he has this bag and I know it's full of things for me, he's bringing me all these things he thinks I'll like for my birthday. It's very sweet, he's like a little dog. When a cat brings you a mouse. I watch him crossing the park and that right there is a moment when – what is it? Well I knew for sure anyway, I felt so big with the feeling. What was it? He gets to me and we both sit down. But we can't have had a cup of tea. I don't think we'd gone to a tea shop. Oh, no. We were in a park. And that was a favourite place of ours, we used to lie down in there, I let him be very fast. I didn't worry, because I knew. What was I – ? I can see him walking in and out of the light across the park with his face sometimes dappled and his face sometimes clear. I wish I could put my finger on it. Put a pin in my life and say, this is the moment I became myself. This is the scene my life was about. Can I go now? Can I go? Can I go now? I need the toilet.

Enter STEPHEN, carrying a dish cloth, drying his hands.

STEPHEN: All right old crone?

EDIE: Yes.

STEPHEN: Do you need the loo?

EDIE: No, it's the only way is all.

STEPHEN: Only way what?

EDIE: If I just call you don't come. You'll only look after me if I threaten to pee on the armchairs.

STEPHEN: How are you feeling?

EDIE: Did you like your tea?

STEPHEN: I loved it.

EDIE: Did you?

STEPHEN: I did, I loved it.

EDIE: Do you cook at home?

STEPHEN: Sometimes. Emily does most of the cooking.

EDIE: She's a good cook is she?

STEPHEN: Great.

EDIE: I've begun a project in the kitchen.

STEPHEN: Oh yeah?

EDIE: I don't cook all the old things any more. I threw Mary Berry away. I'm learning to cook new dishes.

STEPHEN: Like what?

EDIE: Oh, anything really. I buy new cook books. Yotam Ottolenghi. A cook book from London I tried to learn falafels out of.

STEPHEN: Falafels, Mum.

EDIE: Is it? I thought it was falafels. Anyway, they were impossible. Flour and beans, we got past that in the fifties.

STEPHEN: I like falafels.

EDIE: You should try mine. Your Dad wouldn't touch them.

STEPHEN: I would have loved them, I bet they were marvellous.

EDIE: I think you are like a psychopath, because you're very charming.

STEPHEN: Why does that make me a psychopath?

EDIE: Psychopaths are charming. And I don't want to be mad on my own.

STEPHEN: You're not mad, Mum.

EDIE: That's what it feels like, going mad. I've seen people further down the line than me. They reach for words. They'll point at a glass of water and say 'can you pass me the – the the the the / the the…'

STEPHEN: All right, not now Mum yeah? Let's not think about that right now.

EDIE: I'm only messing about.

STEPHEN: It's harder for us, you know.

EDIE: It's not.

STEPHEN: It will be eventually. You won't know your arse from your elbow and we'll still be in love with you, won't we.

EDIE: I couldn't love anyone who thought their elbows were their –

STEPHEN: No, well. What do you think of her?

EDIE: Who?

STEPHEN: Kate.

EDIE: Who?

STEPHEN: Kate, Mum, the girl we – at dinner – are you joking?

EDIE: Course I am.

STEPHEN: Mum!

EDIE: I'd forgotten her name, I knew she was here though.

STEPHEN: Thank God for that.

EDIE: God's got nothing to do with it.

STEPHEN: Sorry. You can say Thank God if you mean it can't you?

EDIE: Yes, but you don't mean it.

STEPHEN: Mother! Do you like her?

EDIE: She seems nice.

STEPHEN: But she's such a good idea, isn't she? She's going to be such a help?

EDIE: I'm sure she is.

STEPHEN: You must be a bit pleased.

EDIE: I'm sorry Steve, I am pleased.

STEPHEN: You have to accept / Dad's got to be out and you –

EDIE: I do.

Enter KATE.

KATE: All done.

STEPHEN: We were just talking about you.

KATE: Yeah?

EDIE: He thinks I'm not pleased enough.

STEPHEN: Mum.

KATE: Aren't you?

EDIE: Oh, I'm happy, of course I'm happy. I just wonder about dying, don't I.

STEPHEN: Mum.

KATE: That's natural.

EDIE: I know. He doesn't, but you and I do.

KATE: That's why we'll get on. We can wonder about dying together.

EDIE: I don't think it need concern you yet.

KATE: I get so obsessed though. Last year, I was reading this poem and you know? I just suddenly knew with this amazing – certainty, that I was going to die. I mean, definitely die. I freaked man, I didn't sleep for weeks after. I couldn't believe it.

STEPHEN: You always knew it was going to happen though?

KATE: Yeah. But I never knew knew, you know?

STEPHEN: Hardest two questions my girls have asked me. First was, where do we go when we die?

EDIE: Oh yes.

STEPHEN: You can't believe it when they ask you! It happens so young.

KATE: How old were they?

STEPHEN: Hannah was four or five or something? So I'm twenty – what? I'm in my twenties. And this kid comes up to you and asks, where do we go when we die? Well I don't know, do I. And I've had no advice on what you're meant to say when that happens. That's not in the baby manuals! If you're, if you're like me and you think there's nothing –

EDIE: Oh –

STEPHEN: Sorry Mum – if you think there's nothing then isn't it your moral – obligation to say that? Otherwise you're going to have to lie to this child and later they're going to know you lied to them. But if you say to a child, there's nothing after you die, your life just ends, aren't you going to freak her out? So Hannah asks me and all this is rushing through my head and I'm thinking, what's the youngest ever recorded suicide? It's like, Jude the Obscure isn't it? Could you do that to a kid if you tell her there's nothing after death? And then you start thinking, what if I'm wrong? Do I have a right to rule out the possibility of faith in this kid's life? I've hardly ever been right about anything. What if I'm wrong and she thinks there's no point in being good and misbehaves all her life and then she dies and it turns out there is a heaven, and she has to go to hell because I told her there was no point in behaving?

KATE: What did you say?

STEPHEN: I was so confused, I just said, I don't know. And Hannah nodded, she looked really serious and said, I see. So I thought, great, she's fallen for that as an actual answer. So I got into it a bit and I said, I don't think we can know. And she said great, thanks Dad. And then she walked off.

KATE: So you have two / daughters?

STEPHEN: Yeah. Hannah and Sam. Samantha, we all call her Sam. She insists.

EDIE: And she gets what she wants!

STEPHEN: They're growing up now, fifteen and thirteen, they're impossible. D'you wanna see a picture?

KATE: Sure.

EDIE: Have you got a picture?

STEPHEN: Yeah.

EDIE: Can I see it too?

STEPHEN: Of course, sorry, of course.

EDIE: Oh, lovely. Don't they look lovely. Doesn't Hannah look like her mother now?

STEPHEN: Scowling.

EDIE: Will of her own.

STEPHEN: Mum and Emily don't get on.

EDIE: Why would you tell her that? What have I said?

STEPHEN: Will of her own? Come off it. I'm just explaining why you went all –

EDIE: There's nothing to explain. Emma's just –

STEPHEN: Emily.

EDIE: That's right.

KATE: Here's your –

STEPHEN: Thanks.

EDIE: She's got a will of her own is all, she's a strong woman.

KATE: So Hannah's doing her GCSEs?

STEPHEN: Just started, yeah. It's so strange. You remember doing them yourself, you know?

KATE: Yeah.

EDIE: GCSEs were yesterday for her.

KATE: Well, six years.

STEPHEN: I did O levels.

EDIE: What did the O stand for?

STEPHEN: God knows.

KATE: Are they at the same school?

STEPHEN: No. Hannah got into the grammar, Sam didn't, so she goes to the comp. It's hard. I don't think Sam cares. Yet. Hannah does. And we do.

KATE: Yeah?

STEPHEN: We stayed where we are because of the grammar school. Otherwise we might have lived anywhere, we both do work that could happen pretty much anywhere.

KATE: What do you – ?

STEPHEN: I'm in insurance. Emily works down in Southampton, at the university.

KATE: She's an academic?

STEPHEN: No, administrative work. So we feel like the girls going to different schools is our fault really.

KATE: What's the other hardest question you've been asked?

EDIE: Oh, that's the obvious.

KATE: What?

EDIE: Where do babies come from.

STEPHEN: Yeah.

KATE: Oh right.

STEPHEN: Where do babies come from Daddy? Can I have one? Can I have one, she said.

KATE: How old?

STEPHEN: Hannah was – five or six, I guess. She worked out dying before she worked out sex. I don't know whether that's good or bad.

EDIE: What a strange question.

KATE: What did you say?

STEPHEN: Well I knew you were supposed to start with, 'when a man and a woman love each other very much'. So I said that. And then I thought, I've never heard this speech. Dad never did it. I didn't know what you were meant to say next. I mean, what do you actually say? So I said, they get together and make a baby.

EDIE: And then it grows in the Mummy's tummy and when it's ready it comes out.

STEPHEN: Yeah. It was so scary. There was a second where I really was about to say to my five-year-old child, when a man and a woman love each other very much they fuck each other.

EDIE: Potty mouth.

STEPHEN: Sorry Mum.

EDIE: Your language is appalling / Stephen.

STEPHEN: Mum thinks saying God or Jesus is swearing.

EDIE: I don't think it is, I know it is! It is swearing!

STEPHEN: Sorry.

EDIE: That's enough of this. I'd like to go to bed.

STEPHEN: I was only –

EDIE: It's all right. Will you help me up?

KATE: I'll help you.

STEPHEN: I don't mind –

KATE: Why don't we get into the habit?

EDIE: Are you sure?

KATE: I'd like to.

EDIE: Well thank you. Is the washing up done?

KATE: Yeah. Come on, show me where your room is.

EDIE: All right.

STEPHEN: Thanks.

EDIE: Night Steve, love to the girls.

STEPHEN: Night Mum.

Enter ARTHUR.

ARTHUR: That's the chickens in.

EDIE: Have you locked up the chickens?

ARTHUR: Just done. Sly buggers.

EDIE: They are, they are.

ARTHUR: Off to bed?

EDIE: Yes.

ARTHUR: Is Kate going to take you?

KATE: Is that all right?

EDIE: Of course it is, he's just talking to me like I'm a baby.

ARTHUR: I'm not!

EDIE: You are, that was baby talk. You patronise me now I'm going senile.

ARTHUR: Well you patronised me all my life.

EDIE: I did not. I just talked very slowly because you're thick.

ARTHUR: All right. Night you.

EDIE: Good night love.

KATE: Down in a minute.

Exit KATE and EDIE.

STEPHEN: Good dinner, right?

ARTHUR: Oh, yeah? Cous cous. I mean, really. I've never known anything took longer to get through or gave less pleasure.

STEPHEN: She likes it.

ARTHUR: Mediterranean stuffed peppers. Waste of cheese. I hate running round like that in that yard.

STEPHEN: You shouldn't keep chickens.

ARTHUR: Your mother likes them.

STEPHEN: Yeah.

ARTHUR: What?

STEPHEN: She won't want them much longer, will she?

ARTHUR: Right.

ARTHUR starts to rearrange and tidy the furniture.

STEPHEN: Wanna hear a joke?

ARTHUR: What?

STEPHEN: Wanna hear a joke?

ARTHUR: Go on then.

STEPHEN: This old bloke dies, and he gets to the pearly gates and St Paul says sorry mate, we're full up, have to try the other place. So he goes to hell, and Satan meets him at the door and says come on in, always room for one more! So he gets ushered in, and Satan takes his coat and says, actually, this is your lucky day, we've been trialling a new customer-oriented management model here, because we're so uncompetitive in terms of attracting guests and our board really don't see why everyone in the history of the world should always want to go to the room upstairs. So you've still come to hell, but that doesn't have to be the worst news you've ever had, oh no. We're putting people's fates back in their own hands. Today I'm going to give you a choice of how you'd like to spend the rest of eternity, because our board know that customers value choice. That's the lesson of the free market – choice, choice, choice, and when we did our market research we found there was nothing on earth people associated more closely with Satan than the free market. Except perhaps genocide. But I'm quite busy today, we've got a lot of new visitors, so if it's all right with you I'll give you a choice of three.

So the bloke says, OK, sounds good, lead on Macduff. So Satan opens a grille in a door and shows him a room. In the room, there's a lake of fire with men drowning in it. Your standard model, he says, pretty average day in hell. Bloke says OK, what's next? And in the next room he sees lots of blokes strapped to rocks having their stomachs eaten by vultures and then growing back to be eaten again. Bit of a classical reference, Satan says, for the sophisticated sufferer. Bloke nods, he'd like to see the last one please. And in the third room, he sees a lot of men standing around waist-deep in shit, sipping coffee. They've all got little cups of coffee, with little saucers, and they're in like a swimming pool of shit. There's a devil imp lifeguard at one end, and all these blokes just standing around. So the bloke says this one looks much better, I'll do this! I mean, it smells, but it's better than fire or getting eaten alive, and you get something to drink. So Satan shows him in, says have a nice afterlife, and the bloke stands in the shit with the others. It's a bit squelchy, it stinks, but he thinks, I have so won here, this is much better. Then suddenly a whistle goes. And the little lifeguard imp says right, break's over, see you in five hundred years – back on your heads!

ARTHUR: St Peter.

STEPHEN: What?

ARTHUR: It's St Peter guards the pearly gates. 'And I will give unto thee the keys of the kingdom of heaven: and whatsoever thou shalt bind on earth shall be bound in heaven: and whatsoever thou shalt loose on earth shall be loosed in heaven.' Matthew 16:19.

STEPHEN: Right.

ARTHUR: You staying?

STEPHEN: I've got to get back.

Silence.

Act Two

SCENE ONE

EDIE is sitting, unable to see STEPHEN, who is standing in the doorway. She sings Celine Dion's 'Only Girl In The World'. KATE enters, singing at the top of her voice, a plate of cake in each hand. Sees STEPHEN and stops.

KATE: Oh.

STEPHEN: That's a truly horrible noise Mum.

EDIE: Who's there?

STEPHEN: Me, idiot.

KATE: Stephen.

EDIE: Who's there?

STEPHEN: The bloke you shag on Wednesdays.

EDIE: Oh you.

KATE: It's good for her.

STEPHEN: Why?

KATE: She likes it.

EDIE: It's nice.

KATE: She remembers the words.

STEPHEN: I just wish you had better taste.

EDIE: I've got wonderful taste!

KATE: What do you like anyway? Old man music I reckon.

STEPHEN: Depeche Mode are brilliant. I bet you listen to the folk revival and pretend you enjoy it.

KATE: Cake?

KATE leaves.

STEPHEN: Lovely. God I'm stiff from the car.

EDIE: What are you doing?

STEPHEN: Stretches. Chiro said it's good for me. Don't look, I get embarrassed.

EDIE: So you should. What are you doing here anyway?

STEPHEN: I had a meeting in glamorous Swindon, I thought I'd take a detour on the way back and see you.

EDIE: Ooh aren't we lucky?

KATE: Do you often have meetings in Swindon?

STEPHEN: Meetings are all people in Swindon have.

KATE: Really?

STEPHEN: It's just office after office after office, yeah. It's the life insurance capital of the world.

EDIE: Really?

STEPHEN: No, that's probably Zurich. But Swindon's like a close third, it's the big thing there. That and prostitution.

KATE: Seriously?

STEPHEN: Sort of goes with the meetings. There's a lot of trade from the company cars. They line up on the commercial roads like welcome parties.

EDIE: How distasteful.

STEPHEN: Swindon is like the Vietnam of the insurance industry. No one wants to go, but you have to go because that's where everything's happening. Then once you get there there are millions of prostitutes. But we have Paolo Di Canio running the football club instead of Robin Williams running the radio station. Which is basically the same thing.

STEPHEN exits.

EDIE: What's he doing?

STEPHEN: Sorry?

EDIE: What's he want, why's he come here?

KATE: He was just dropping by to see you.

EDIE: Don't fall for that, I know him, he wants something. Turning up like that.

KATE: Edie –

EDIE: I bet you've come to take me, has he come to take me? I don't want to go into a home. I won't know where I am.

Enter STEPHEN.

KATE: I'm sure it's nothing like that. Be calm. It's fine.

EDIE: So you just thought you'd drop by?

STEPHEN: Yeah. That OK?

EDIE: It's lovely. You've never done it before.

STEPHEN: I have.

EDIE: When?

STEPHEN: I don't know, but in the last, twenty years I will have dropped by.

EDIE: Will you.

STEPHEN: I didn't have any more meetings. I thought you'd be pleased to see me.

EDIE: Yes.

STEPHEN: But you're not.

EDIE: No, just surprised is all.

KATE: What is it you do, exactly? You're a sort of salesman, I guess? Not in a bad way, I just mean –

STEPHEN: Well –

KATE: More than the money side, / anyway.

EDIE: Terrible / at maths.

STEPHEN: Yeah. I'm in the human side.

KATE: Do you have to spend a lot of time talking to – dying people?

EDIE: Only when he comes here.

KATE: Edie.

STEPHEN: Those calls happen lower down. I manage the people who make them. Sometimes I get involved in difficult cases.

KATE: What's a difficult case in life insurance?

STEPHEN: Well, I guess – *(He nods to EDIE, who has started to hum very quietly.)*

KATE: You what?

STEPHEN: Sometimes people are insured. And they have a type of cover which might pay out if they get a certain type of illness. Like, cancer. But the guidelines on dementia make for problem cases. In a way, in a technical, legal way, someone with dementia's already dead –

KATE: Whoa –

STEPHEN: No, because it's got you, and it's going to get you completely. It's just about timing. So if I was – if you were related to someone in that situation, you could go to your insurers and say, look, if I go NHS for her care, by the time someone comes free to visit her every now and then and check she's watering her flowers she's going to be on life support. So will you pay out now so I can make her comfortable? And that would be a problem case.

KATE: Why?

STEPHEN: Because right now you can't call this a terminal illness, can you. So if I were making the judgement I wouldn't pay out. She hasn't crossed the line yet, she hasn't started actually dying, she's just old.

EDIE: You've forgotten to pretend you're not talking about me.

STEPHEN: Oh, Mum, I'm –

EDIE: It's all right. It's the council that's the pirate.

KATE: Why?

EDIE: Two years maybe before they can help you. Or you can accelerate the process if you try to kill yourself a certain number of times.

KATE: Seriously?

EDIE: I wouldn't. I used to say when I start to go gaga get the gun and shoot me, but when push comes to shove you want to stick around as long as you can.

KATE: Of course.

STEPHEN: I put Mum on a waiting list before you came. But we don't know how long it'll be.

EDIE: I wouldn't need it either.

STEPHEN: You would, it'd be someone doing everything Kate's doing and she does enough, doesn't she?

EDIE: We have Kate.

STEPHEN: I didn't know that when I put your name down, did I! Sorry. Being here sets my teeth on edge.

EDIE: Well I'm sorry for that.

STEPHEN: No, I – forget it. Where's Dad?

EDIE: Out in the fields.

STEPHEN: Course.

EDIE: He'll be hours yet. He'd be hopeless if I went into care, you know that Stephen don't you? You'd have to move in here.

STEPHEN: I couldn't, Mum.

EDIE: He wouldn't cope. You'd have to sell the farm and put him in with me. I get so scared when I think of leaving him alone and he never learned to do anything round the house.

STEPHEN: He'll be all right. He'll live twenty years to spite me.

EDIE: He's not trying to spite you! He's just no good at talking. Neither are you.

KATE: So – how are Emily and Hannah and Sam?

STEPHEN: Erm, fine, yeah. I've been travelling too much. Haven't seen enough of them. Half the time in London.

EDIE: The Somme of the insurance world. Everyone marching willingly into the field to have their lives taken away from them.

STEPHEN: It's not all bad.

EDIE: You can't fool me, I've seen how much those paninis cost.

STEPHEN: Emily thinks I crack jokes all the time to try and be like you.

EDIE: Does she? I suppose she's just trying to make you feel bad.

STEPHEN: You what?

EDIE: She always does, takes the fun out of everything.

STEPHEN: Jesus, Mum.

EDIE: Well I don't know why someone who tells a joke should have to be subjected to psychological analysis afterwards.

STEPHEN: My jokes are shit Mum, she can't exactly laugh at them, she has to say something.

EDIE: No, that's true, you don't tell the sort of jokes that are actually funny.

STEPHEN: Just the sort of jokes that make me look desperate to impress people and hopelessly insecure.

KATE: Do you think that?

STEPHEN: No, that was a joke, I think – well actually I think I fish for sympathy. Look, I'm doing it now, it's working, you're feeling sorry for me. People feel sorry for people who tell shit jokes.

KATE: Why do you want sympathy?

STEPHEN: I don't quite mean – I mean I want people to like me.

EDIE: He's always been insecure. Never had proper friends at school, never brought anyone home. Not a socialiser. When he was in junior school he told us some of the boys in his class were bullying him. We asked him what was happening. He said at breaktimes he'd walk around this white line telling himself a story, this painted line on the field above the classrooms. And at each end of the field these boys would shout at him. We asked him, when they shout at you, are you walking past some posts with a net hanging off them? And he said yes. So we told him you're walking round a football pitch, they're shouting at you because you're in front of the goal. Never been good with people, have you? Off in your own world.

STEPHEN: Thanks for that. I wish you'd go senile faster.

EDIE: That's cos you don't know about all the gambling debts you're going to inherit.

STEPHEN: Ho ho ho.

KATE: You should see someone if you feel like that about yourself.

STEPHEN: What, therapy?

KATE: I got therapy. I thought it was brilliant.

STEPHEN: Oh –

KATE: What?

STEPHEN: Well, you aside, right? But I just think, come off it. I'm living one of the best lives anyone's ever lived. I've got clean running water, my BCG, a job and kids and all my limbs, I don't need –

EDIE: Do you think you're being a bit close-minded?

STEPHEN: Therapy's for people who've been trained to think they're important by watching too much TV.

KATE: If it helps, it helps, is all –

STEPHEN: That's what fat people say when they allow themselves a biscuit.

KATE: Right.

STEPHEN: Sorry. Don't you think?

KATE: I don't know.

EDIE: I think you do.

KATE: No, actually you're right Edie, I do, of course our lives are lucky next to other people's. But the way you feel isn't relative to how other people feel, is it, it's about how you feel. It's not your fault if you're living small and your problems look trivial. That's actually half the problem.

STEPHEN: Right. Sorry.

KATE: There's nothing to apologise for.

STEPHEN: No but I am, I'm sorry.

EDIE: That's Emily as well, he apologises for everything, never used to do that.

STEPHEN: Mum.

EDIE: Well it's true, isn't it?

STEPHEN: I don't know, Mum. Let's just agree with what you think. But there are a lot of things I never used to do when I lived here. I never used to have anyone to talk to. I never used to feel able to do what I wanted and get the bus into town.

EDIE: I would have liked for you to have had someone to play with as much as you.

STEPHEN: I'm sorry, I'm snapping. We're bickerers in this family. Emily and me haven't had the chance to actually, properly, see each other in too long, so it's just a bit of a sore –

EDIE: Oh.

STEPHEN: No, it's nothing, it's just you talking about her when I feel a bit –

EDIE: Oh.

STEPHEN: Emily's good for me, you see. She sees through all – this. Chatter chatter chatter. Punctures the bubble, that's good for me. But I get back late, she gets back late, we're already asleep when the other one gets home, or whatever – you can miss people even when they're around, you know. It's all fine, Mum, it's just a bit – you know.

EDIE: Sorry.

STEPHEN: No, no.

EDIE: I do think you're unhappy though.

KATE: I had a boyfriend once was never there even when he was with me. He wanted to be a poet. He was always thinking somewhere else. It was torture really. He was in the room but then he wasn't at the same time.

EDIE: We're not our bodies, are we, we're just in them.

STEPHEN: Excuse me?

EDIE: We're not our lives either. We're just in them. We bob about and bump into each other and our lives and our bodies slip past us.

STEPHEN: You all right? You sound like a new age mental.

EDIE: Just thinking.

STEPHEN: Like you're trying to interest me in homeopathy.

KATE: I actually get a lot from homeopathy.

STEPHEN: Seriously?

KATE: No.

STEPHEN: Thank God for that. People who like homeopathy are write-offs. You know how sometimes you just know you're not going to get on with certain people?

KATE: Anyone who likes the folk revival.

STEPHEN: Anyone who listens to flute rock at least.

EDIE: But what is it anyway, this – why are we all tied up in this?

STEPHEN: You all right Mum?

EDIE: Do you feel you're off-target? I do. Bogged down in all this – living. I don't know what I was aiming for, I know I missed it. I didn't get one thing right. Crosswords, nothing that mattered.

STEPHEN: That's not true.

EDIE: No?

STEPHEN: It's not.

EDIE: All falls away though, doesn't it. Tide goes out on us. I'm sorry I'm prattling, I get so depressed. But when I say it out loud, I mean, it's important to me, it's my life, it's the most important thing in the world to me, but it's so mundane. I'm acting like it might matter to someone. And yet I feel I'm underwater.

STEPHEN: Do you need a rest, or –

KATE starts singing 'All Coming Back To Me Now'. EDIE joins in.

STEPHEN: Sorry I was stressing you out.

EDIE: No, I manage that all by myself, you're all right.

KATE: Cup of tea?

EDIE: That'd be lovely.

KATE: D'you want one?

STEPHEN: Thanks.

KATE: Where's your –

STEPHEN: Oh, here. Kate?

KATE: Yeah?

STEPHEN: I was thinking we should go for a drink some time. I meant to say that, while I remember, erm. We should go for a drink, get you out of the house, sort of thing.

KATE: Oh. OK.

STEPHEN: If you fancy it.

KATE: Yeah, that'd be great. Yeah.

STEPHEN: Maybe next weekend or –

KATE: OK.

STEPHEN: Great.

KATE: I'll just get the –

Exit KATE.

EDIE: I hope that was a sensible thing you just did.

STEPHEN: Sorry?

EDIE: You know very well.

STEPHEN: I –

EDIE: It's all right, leave it.

STEPHEN: I really don't know what you mean.

EDIE: People are like glass. You see through them, you never get to them.

STEPHEN: What do you mean?

EDIE: I mean because I'm your mother I've always been able to see what you were thinking. But I don't think I've ever got you to talk to me about it once.

STEPHEN: We talk.

EDIE: There's talking and talking. The worst thing about all this is having to give up on projects I haven't even started getting to grips with.

STEPHEN: Meaning –

EDIE: I mean what if I die and I still haven't managed to have even one conversation with you.

Enter KATE.

KATE: Kettle's on.

EDIE: Who's she?

STEPHEN: Mum.

EDIE: Stephen, who's this, your friend?

KATE: Edie, it's me, it's Kate.

STEPHEN: Mum are you joking?

EDIE: She's a bit young for you Steve.

KATE: I don't think she can –

EDIE: Sorry, have we met before?

KATE: I think she's forgotten me.

EDIE: We've met before.

KATE: Yes.

EDIE: Oh. Oh yes. Sorry. I remember.

SCENE TWO

EDIE and ARTHUR are sitting in chairs, STEPHEN is standing. ARTHUR has a bit of a tractor on his lap.

STEPHEN: Funny driving through town on the way up, I recognised almost everyone.

ARTHUR: Pat Owen had a story, did you know Pat? Went away when he was young, farmed elsewhere and never came home for forty years. When he did come back, twenty years ago now maybe, he got off the bus feeling the whole world was going to stop for him, like something real was happening, and an old boy sitting on the fence looked up and said hello Pat, haven't seen you in a while. And that was it. I imagine he took a draw on his pipe. Faces never change here. Except yours. So what do you want to talk about?

STEPHEN: Well –

ARTHUR: Can you help? It's a fiddle.

STEPHEN: Sure, what do I –

ARTHUR: Just sort of – I need you to hold this flush – OK?

STEPHEN: Yep.

ARTHUR: Right.

STEPHEN: Is your lap the best place, or –

ARTHUR: We could do it on the floor?

STEPHEN: Shall we do that?

ARTHUR: Yep.

STEPHEN: There you go.

ARTHUR: So the thing is it won't be level if you let it touch the floor, you have to hold it up so it's like, proud like –

STEPHEN: Got it.

EDIE: Can I help?

ARTHUR: You're all right. Right. So what do you want to talk about?

STEPHEN: Well, I was talking to Kate last week, did you know I popped in last week?

ARTHUR: Oh yeah.

STEPHEN: We were talking about – insurance. Because I'm a fascinating conversationalist, and we kind of revisited something you and I have talked about before, but things I hadn't thought about in a little –

ARTHUR: Careful.

STEPHEN: What?

ARTHUR: It's not –

STEPHEN: It'll be all right when it tightens.

ARTHUR: Not if you hold it like that.

STEPHEN: OK, so what –

ARTHUR: A bit more – yep. That'll do it. Go on.

STEPHEN: Well we were talking about early payouts. Do you remember we talked about that before?

ARTHUR: Oh yeah.

STEPHEN: And I was telling her how difficult it was to get one, but while I was driving home I got to thinking about Mum's –

ARTHUR: Hopeless.

STEPHEN: What?

ARTHUR: See. I've done too many, my hand's too tired.

STEPHEN: Why don't you hold and I'll screw? As the bishop said to the actress.

ARTHUR: What?

STEPHEN: Nothing. Why don't we swap?

ARTHUR: Do you think you could get it in properly?

STEPHEN: There you go again.

ARTHUR: What?

STEPHEN: Nothing.

EDIE: Are you fighting?

ARTHUR: No. Can you do it?

STEPHEN: I'll have a go.

ARTHUR: Come round here and I'll go round there.

STEPHEN: OK. This one?

ARTHUR: Yep.

STEPHEN: So I went back to – Mum's documents, basically, when I got home. And the thing is, I got her a pretty good – policy. How's that?

ARTHUR: Bit more.

STEPHEN: And I reckon I could get some money now if I set my mind to it. You know, get her properly looked after.

ARTHUR: Oh.

STEPHEN: So I thought I'd talk to you.

ARTHUR: Right.

STEPHEN: How's that?

ARTHUR: That's it.

He gets up and picks up the part.

STEPHEN: Where are you going?

ARTHUR: I'll just put it back on while there's some –

STEPHEN: Right.

ARTHUR: OK?

STEPHEN: I just thought we were talking about –

ARTHUR: Yeah. I'll just do this then we can talk.

STEPHEN: OK.

Exit ARTHUR.

STEPHEN: You all right Mum?

EDIE: Tired.

STEPHEN: Oh yeah. Where's Kate?

EDIE: Out.

STEPHEN: Do you want a drink, or –

EDIE: No.

STEPHEN: Have you had an OK day?

EDIE: No. I need –

STEPHEN: What?

EDIE: I need, erm – *(She gestures to her chair.)*

STEPHEN: What do you mean, Mum, are you uncomfortable?

EDIE: Yeah.

STEPHEN: OK. Let's move you a bit then, would that help? Come on.

EDIE: Yeah.

STEPHEN: You're sitting on – you're sitting on all carrier bags.

EDIE: Yeah.

STEPHEN: What are you doing that for? Course you're uncomfortable, you're all –

Enter ARTHUR.

ARTHUR: It's no good, my eyes, we left it too late. I'll have to do it in the morning.

STEPHEN: Why's Mum sitting on all these carrier bags?

ARTHUR: In case she forgets to go to the toilet.

STEPHEN: Does that happen?

ARTHUR: Just a couple of times. And I'm out all day and Kate had to go to do the shopping, so –

STEPHEN: But she's started –

ARTHUR: A bit.

STEPHEN: Oh –

EDIE: Sorry.

STEPHEN: No, no, Mum –

ARTHUR: She's all right while Kate's here.

STEPHEN: Yeah. But we need to make a plan, Dad, she's getting worse so fast.

ARTHUR: She's fine.

STEPHEN: But she's –

ARTHUR: I know. I know.

STEPHEN: Strange how men get shy when they don't want to talk.

ARTHUR: Strange how men never want to talk to each other.

STEPHEN: Shall we sit down?

ARTHUR: OK.

They sit.

STEPHEN: So I think I could get some money for care.

EDIE: What?

STEPHEN: Don't worry, Mum.

ARTHUR: Could she be looked after here?

STEPHEN: Maybe.

ARTHUR: Just –

STEPHEN: It depends what she needs, they'd make an assessment.

ARTHUR: So you'd just move her –

STEPHEN: No, Dad, I'm just trying to be realistic. Some time soon, I'm really sorry but the way things are going some time soon –

ARTHUR: Could I go with her?

STEPHEN: Maybe. Some places do that. Do you want to?

ARTHUR: I don't want her to go. I don't want to sell the farm.

STEPHEN: We maybe wouldn't need to sell the farm if I got –

ARTHUR: But there's no point havin it if she's not here. You wouldn't want it.

STEPHEN: No, but you could come back when –

ARTHUR: I couldn't. I couldn't.

STEPHEN: The other thing is, Dad, it might not be possible for you to go with her. We'll need to be ready for that. Some places do it but not everywhere, OK?

ARTHUR: I'd rather put it off as late as we can then.

STEPHEN: What do you mean?

ARTHUR: I'd rather she was here until she absolutely couldn't be.

STEPHEN: Even if that wasn't the best for Mum?

ARTHUR: What d'you mean, it's her home, it's our life, of course it's best for her!

EDIE: Sssh, boys.

ARTHUR: Sorry love. Of course it's best.

STEPHEN: Even if a nurse said –

ARTHUR: I'm pretty sure she's going to keep wanting to be here till she absolutely can't be, all right? That's all.

STEPHEN: OK. I think I probably need to make you aware of something else too. Not a – just something that might be relevant. Erm, Emily and me are having trouble. And she's kind of said to me, kind of that she's not sure we should be together. Or married. And we're kind of talking about me moving out, because we – fight, and it upsets the kids, and they have exams, you know?

ARTHUR: Right.

STEPHEN: And I'm just telling you this because it might mean my life's about to change quite a lot. And I'm not sure how, but right now I'm visiting a lot, and I don't know – and it's on my mind that Kate might not be here for ever, and if she leaves and I can't help and you're having to put down carrier bags already –

EDIE: It was my idea the bags. I told him to get them.

STEPHEN: Oh yeah?

EDIE: Good idea.

STEPHEN: Absolutely, yeah.

ARTHUR: I'm sorry about you and Emily, Steve.

STEPHEN: Oh. Thanks.

ARTHUR: I mean, yeah. Do you think it's a passing thing, or –

STEPHEN: I don't know really.

ARTHUR: How are you feeling about it?

STEPHEN: Erm. Underwater.

ARTHUR: Right. I can see what you're saying. I can see it affects – we do know you come here as much as you can, we do appreciate it.

STEPHEN: Well –

ARTHUR: If it helps, she's never been good enough for you. I've never liked her. I mean, it might not be the worst thing that happened, you know?

STEPHEN: Right.

ARTHUR: Is that the wrong thing –

STEPHEN: She's the mother of my children and I've been married to her for almost twenty years.

ARTHUR: Right. Sorry. Yeah.

STEPHEN: Can we get back to –

ARTHUR: Yeah. So you want to –

STEPHEN: Look into getting the insurance money.

ARTHUR: I guess that makes –

STEPHEN: Yeah?

ARTHUR: Do we need to start thinking about selling the farm?

STEPHEN: Do you want to?

ARTHUR: I don't want to be here once she's not.

STEPHEN: Are you sure? You love it here.

ARTHUR: No. Only the people living on it. Only the life here, not the place. I'd go.

STEPHEN: Would you?

ARTHUR: It's too – it'd be too –

STEPHEN: Yeah.

EDIE: You wouldn't sell it would you?

ARTHUR: Don't worry love, we're talking hypothetically.

EDIE: Did they go bust or have enough, the Joneses, which was it? Or did they just get old?

STEPHEN: What if we met an estate agent then?

ARTHUR: I know what he'd say.

STEPHEN: What?

ARTHUR: That no one'll want it. Farming like it is, housing like it is, no one'll want this. I'm under no illusions about what I've got here.

STEPHEN: Don't feel sorry for yourself.

ARTHUR: I'm sorry, but it's hard not to. You look at a wheat field all your life. It's a beautiful view, how it changes as the year rolls round. But at the same time it's not much of the world, is it. Now I'm getting left here. I just wish it was me it happened to.

STEPHEN: Yeah. Yeah, me too.

SCENE THREE

EDIE is alone on stage.

EDIE: Ever watch the light cross this wall? Outline of the window crossing that stone, that's the whole earth spinning, whole lives changing. You can watch it all from here. In my dream he comes to me and we say all these things we've never said to each other before. And he's happy.

Enter STEPHEN.

STEPHEN: You on your own?

EDIE: You're all dressed up.

STEPHEN: Erm –

EDIE: Smart.

STEPHEN: Yeah. Is Kate –

EDIE: What?

STEPHEN: Upstairs?

EDIE: I don't know. Are you all dressed up for her?

STEPHEN: No.

EDIE: Are you?

STEPHEN: No.

EDIE: Why?

STEPHEN: Mum, I'm not dressed up, don't worry about it.

EDIE: Have you got a date? You never had a date.

STEPHEN: Mum –

Enter KATE.

KATE: All right?

STEPHEN: Fine thanks. You?

KATE: Yeah.

STEPHEN: Great. Still on for tonight?

KATE: I can't, I'm sorry.

STEPHEN: Oh.

KATE: I can't go out tonight.

STEPHEN: Oh. OK.

KATE: I think you might have said something before I came
      home and found a for sale sign on the driveway.

STEPHEN: What?

EDIE: What are you selling?

KATE: I'm not saying it's anything to do with – but I am living
      here, you might have said.

STEPHEN: About selling the house?

KATE: Yeah. I didn't know I needed to be making other plans. I do now. But –

STEPHEN: It's going to be ages, we'll never sell it, that's a formality, just –

KATE: Right.

STEPHEN: Is that why you can't come out? I'm sorry, I didn't think, I didn't realise. You were out when me and Dad planned it and then I've been doing it all in Salisbury, I haven't seen you.

KATE: I just got here as well.

STEPHEN: I'm sorry. I didn't think –

KATE: I know it's nothing to do with me. But I just got here. It's like getting chucked.

STEPHEN: No –

KATE: Everyone I ever have anything to do with ends up doing this. It's just so boring, people not thinking of you. I'll have to go.

STEPHEN: No.

KATE: Well I'll have to make plans and I'll have to go when something comes up. I can't hang around here till you kick me out.

STEPHEN: It was never a permanent –

KATE: No, I know. But notice, that's all I want. A bit of warning. So I feel like you thought of me. Which you didn't. I'm sorry. I'm getting so angry, I'm so rude.

STEPHEN: Don't –

KATE: And you're putting your fucking Mum in a home! I don't work so you'll put her in a home.

STEPHEN: Right.

KATE: I'm not saying I feel, I know I was a temporary – but look at her, she's still – how can you do that?

STEPHEN: She's not always going to be –

KATE: No, but how can you just shovel her off like that? And turfing your Dad out of here, how can you do that? And then fucking asking me out in front of your Mum, when you're married, when you have kids my age, and turning up like this? You don't give a fuck about anything.

STEPHEN: I didn't –

KATE: No?

STEPHEN: What?

KATE: Say what you were going to say. You didn't ask me out? You're holding a bunch of flowers.

STEPHEN: They're –

KATE: You've never bought her flowers, there are never flowers in the house.

STEPHEN: Right.

KATE: Look, I'm sorry, I'm being so rude. You're a nice man, you are, and you've sorted me out a bit. But you don't think about anything. I mean how dare you? How can you bump me around like this, sell the house I'm staying in and not think to tell me, then turn up hoping for – what? A snog in your car after you've had too many?

STEPHEN: That's why you're angry.

KATE: All of that is why I'm angry. Because you brought flowers. Because you're having her carted off. Because your Dad wanders round looking lost and frowning at the sign on the drive. Because you're pulling the rug out from under my feet and it's not even important enough for you to notice you're doing it. You're every fucking man I've ever dated.

STEPHEN: I just saw these, I thought they were nice.

KATE: Hopeless. Look, I know I'm being rude talking like this, I know, I will go, I know this is out of order. But you need to hear it man.

STEPHEN: You don't –

KATE: Yeah, I do have to go.

STEPHEN: It's a formality, it's a fucking – so I bought these, yeah. I thought I would, I thought it was a bit bold but I thought I would. Because my wife's filed for a divorce because she's – bored of me, I don't know, and I thought I'd cheer myself up. And that sounds like I'm using you but it doesn't feel like that, I just think you're fun. You're funny. You're beautiful. And I wanted to spend some time with you, and – be around you. I look at you, I think if I could take it all back, do it again, try something different, I would. In a heartbeat. You've still got it in front of you and that's amazing. What have I got? Kids I'll see at weekends. Unfulfilled potential. They have each other. You have the future. So I bought you flowers. And I'm sorry I didn't tell you about Mum or the house, but the thing is, I don't mean to be cruel, but it's nothing really to do with you. You're a visitor here. This is family. It's a family thing.

KATE: It's hard to feel like everything's in front of you if the whole world's just men dropping you when it suits them.

STEPHEN: That's not what's happening. Look, won't you come for a drink? We could talk this over?

KATE: I'm sorry, I can't be bothered, Stephen. I just can't be arsed.

STEPHEN: So what? You're ordering me out of my house?

EDIE: It's not.

STEPHEN: What?

EDIE: You walked out long ago.

Enter ARTHUR.

ARTHUR: Evening all. Hello Steve, you all right?

STEPHEN: Hi.

ARTHUR: Staying for supper?

EDIE: He can't, love.

ARTHUR: Just dropping by? How was your day, love?

EDIE: All right.

ARTHUR: Wouldn't put the kettle on would you Steve? I'm parched.

STEPHEN: I'm sorry, I can't, I've got to go.

ARTHUR: Already?

STEPHEN: I'm sorry. I've got to go.

Exit STEPHEN.

ARTHUR: What was the matter with him?

EDIE: Oh, no. Oh, no no no.

KATE: Are you all right?

EDIE gets up.

EDIE: I don't feel well.

ARTHUR: Is she all right?

EDIE: I remembered the letters.

KATE: What letters Edie?

EDIE: Yesterday, yesterday, didn't I.

KATE: What?

EDIE: I remembered them look.

She picks up a pile of opened letters.

EDIE: They're trying to send me a credit card. They're trying to sell me catalogue. I ought to reply.

ARTHUR: Oh yes.

EDIE: But I had to hide them because I felt so sad.

ARTHUR: What about?

EDIE: Well –

KATE: What made you sad?

EDIE: I just don't think I'll ever go on another holiday.

SCENE FOUR

EDIE, ARTHUR and KATE.

EDIE: Is it today that you're leaving?

KATE: After you've had your lunch.

EDIE: Is Stephen coming to look after us like you?

KATE: Not like –

EDIE: Oh yes. And why have you got so many boxes?

KATE: These aren't for me, these are your things.

EDIE: Why are my things all in boxes?

ARTHUR: It's all right Edie, don't worry.

EDIE: Are we going away? Is it a holiday?

ARTHUR: No, it's not a holiday. Don't you remember I said?

EDIE: What?

ARTHUR: What?

EDIE: Said what?

ARTHUR: Don't you remember I told you what was happening?

EDIE: I give up.

ARTHUR: It's all right, don't worry.

EDIE: It isn't a holiday? That's a shame.

KATE: Can I get you both a cup of tea?

ARTHUR: That would be lovely.

KATE: OK.

Exit KATE.

EDIE: I thought you were unfaithful to me one time.

ARTHUR: Say what?

EDIE: I went into town, not long after we were married, and you were sitting in the window of a hotel with a woman having lunch. I didn't know what to think. I never brought it up, I just came home.

ARTHUR: You didn't think –

EDIE: Not really, no. I've always known you were a good boy. That is your redeeming feature.

ARTHUR: That's what makes me so bloody dull.

EDIE: Yes, you're a straight and narrow road, you.

ARTHUR: What?

EDIE: A straight and narrow road.

ARTHUR: I'm what, Streatham what?

EDIE: A straight and narrow road!

ARTHUR: Oh!

EDIE: Silly.

ARTHUR: My ears.

EDIE: You do make me laugh.

ARTHUR: I don't even remember it. I don't know when you'd be talking about. Sometimes buyers used to meet me with their wives –

EDIE: It's all right. I knew you were a good boy really. I'm only sorry I never asked, it makes it look like I wouldn't have believed you. Perhaps I wouldn't have, I don't know. I believe you now. It's sad, isn't it. Her and Stephen.

ARTHUR: What?

EDIE: Oh, Arthur, really?

ARTHUR: What about her and Stephen?

EDIE: Oh, you are odd. If I felt a bit stronger today I would tell him what he should be doing is leaving his wife. Wouldn't that end up better for both of them? She can't be happy either. Not that I know.

ARTHUR: Actually, they're –

EDIE: What?

ARTHUR: No, no.

EDIE: What?

79

ARTHUR: No, forget it.

EDIE: I probably will.

ARTHUR: I don't know what the point of me would have been if you'd ever left me.

EDIE: No, but we were lucky. We didn't have to think about things like that.

Enter KATE.

EDIE: Are you all right about going away?

KATE: Me?

EDIE: Are you all right about things?

KATE: Well. Yeah, I'm fine. I mean I'm sad, but I'm fine. I'm going to go and look for something else now.

ARTHUR: Do you know what yet?

KATE: No.

ARTHUR: Word of advice?

KATE: Yeah?

ARTHUR: We're in between everything. Nothing ever happens, you shouldn't go looking for that. You'll never stop wanting. The trick is to steer between everything.

EDIE: All you have to do really is get through it all OK and get through to your grave without too much trouble.

KATE: Right. Yeah. I suppose.

EDIE: We were going to have three or four children. One to take over from us and one we thought might teach and we hoped to have a student. We thought we might have a child went into the church, we could have got behind that. But the appetite had gone out of us to be all supporting someone's – what's his name? My son, his name is Stephen. And it was sort of lovely when he married because of course you can live it all again with grandchildren, but it's not the same. Or it wasn't for us. We weren't quite allowed to be involved. You're practically the same age as his children, I don't know what he was thinking, I don't know how he can be so unhappy. I don't know what makes you so unhappy either. I just don't know why you have so many boxes.

ARTHUR: Edie –

Enter STEPHEN.

STEPHEN: Sorry I'm late.

KATE: You OK?

STEPHEN: Yeah. OK. Bad morning.

ARTHUR: We were starting to wonder whether you'd got lost.

STEPHEN: I've come here enough Dad, I wouldn't get lost. You've already done so much packing.

ARTHUR: Up all night.

STEPHEN: I've cleared the whole day –

ARTHUR: It's finished. We can spend the day moving it, can't we.

STEPHEN: Yeah, fine. You look tired.

ARTHUR: Your mother's tired as well.

STEPHEN: Hi Mum, sorry. You OK?

EDIE: I feel quite tired.

KATE: Do you want lunch before I go?

STEPHEN: Are you leaving already?

KATE: I've got to get a train.

STEPHEN: There are trains all day, aren't there?

KATE: I've got to get this one.

ARTHUR: There's the fish pie you cooked for yesterday's dinner, we could have that for lunch?

EDIE: That sounds nice.

KATE: Shall I heat it up?

ARTHUR: Thank you, love.

KATE: I'll be a minute.

Exit KATE.

ARTHUR: OK?

STEPHEN: Yeah, just –

ARTHUR: What's up?

STEPHEN: What do I have to do for you to stop talking to me like that? What have I done that offends you so much?

ARTHUR: What are you / talking –

STEPHEN: You think I'm hopeless.

ARTHUR: No –

STEPHEN: You do, I know you do. It's you two make me a failure. Sitting there together like that, happy like that, what kind of pressure do you think that puts on me?

ARTHUR: Well –

STEPHEN: You look at me like I'm wasting my life. You act like my whole life is a way of trying to disappoint you.

Enter KATE.

KATE: We OK?

STEPHEN: Fine.

KATE: Do you want feeding?

STEPHEN: Are we feeding her now?

EDIE: Yes please.

STEPHEN: Are we feeding –

ARTHUR: I'll do it.

KATE: You sure?

STEPHEN: I didn't know about this.

ARTHUR: Give it here. There we go love.

EDIE: Thank you. I'm sorry.

ARTHUR: I'm sorry too love. There we go. All right.

EDIE: Is this the last meal we'll eat in our house?

ARTHUR: Yes, it is.

EDIE: It seems such a long time we've spent here. But it's not a long time really.

A car beeps.

KATE: That's me. I called a cab.

STEPHEN: I could have given you a lift.

KATE: I didn't want to be any trouble.

STEPHEN: I would have liked to have given you a lift.

KATE: You don't get to try and be friends with me, Stephen. Don't you understand that?

STEPHEN: I was thinking while we drove over the Plain, what would it be like if we did what we wanted, you know? What would happen if I walked out of here, I don't know, if I walked out of here now and left with you?

KATE: That's not what you want.

STEPHEN: No –

KATE: You just don't want to be who you are. I don't know if this occurred to you as being relevant, but it's not what I want either.

ARTHUR: Steve?

STEPHEN: Dad?

ARTHUR: Will you help me up? She's done. My knees.

STEPHEN: Sure. There you go. That's all right.

KATE: Do you want your lunch now Arthur?

Beep.

ARTHUR: Yes please.

KATE: I have to go.

EDIE: Kate?

KATE: Yes?

EDIE: You are very beautiful my love. You bear that in mind, all right? For as long as you're young and can enjoy it you should know that's what's happening to you.

ARTHUR: It's been such a help you being here.

KATE: I'm so sorry that –

Beep.

STEPHEN: Kate.

KATE: Yeah?

STEPHEN: I don't know. Keep in touch?

EDIE: I don't think so, dear.

Exit KATE.

ARTHUR: Can I have my lunch?

STEPHEN: Yeah.

ARTHUR: Then you and I can start packing the car.

STEPHEN: Yeah.

ARTHUR: Any news from the estate agent?

STEPHEN: No, sorry. You ever read any of these?

ARTHUR: They're your mother's. Do you read much?

STEPHEN: A bit.

EDIE: I collected them by subscription.

STEPHEN: Yeah?

EDIE: Bookcase came the same way. Subscription, and they sent a book a month. And a bookcase when you paid your first money, that you one day filled. News from the big world.

STEPHEN: That's a lovely idea.

EDIE: Must be sets like that all over England. Little escapes, little trapdoors out.

ARTHUR: I'd rather go for a walk.

STEPHEN: Did you ever read Trollope?

ARTHUR: No.

STEPHEN: I hated Trollope.

ARTHUR: The Scottish one?

STEPHEN: No, that's Walter Scott. I need to ask you something.

ARTHUR: Oh yeah?

STEPHEN: I was wondering whether it might be helpful if I came and stayed here for a bit. For the first few weeks. Or just while we get it sold, you know? Help you keep it ticking over.

ARTHUR: Joking?

STEPHEN: Why –

ARTHUR: We'll come to blows, Steve, you know we will, are you joking? Why would you want to do that?

STEPHEN: No –

ARTHUR: It's kind of you to think of me but really –

STEPHEN: Actually –

ARTHUR: I know how you feel about this. Me. I don't mind. Or I've come to terms, anyway, heh! I'll be all right, yeah? You just get this place sold and get me somewhere near her.

STEPHEN: Actually Dad Emily's kind of kicked me out of the house. So I was wondering whether I could stay here just while I haven't got anywhere else to go.

ARTHUR: Oh. Right. I see.

STEPHEN: But obviously I did think it would be good, now you're going to be – but maybe while I'm getting it sold I could just sort myself out too, you know?

ARTHUR: Of course. You're always welcome here, Steve, always have been.

EDIE: It's your home.

STEPHEN: Yeah.

EDIE: It's our home.

ARTHUR: All right Edie love. So you'll stay for a bit.

STEPHEN: Thank you.

ARTHUR: OK.

EDIE: Is it nice this place I'm going to?

STEPHEN: Yeah. It's nice.

EDIE: People always used to say we lived out the back of beyond. Will you come and visit me, d'you think?

STEPHEN: As often as I can.

EDIE: And you'll visit me, won't you, Arthur? And look after the house? And remember to change the sheets? And kill the chickens when you move away, don't leave them alone will you? And keep the machines in good nick? What will I do while you're packing?

ARTHUR: *(Goes to her.)* It's all right, my love. I'm going to look after you. It's going to be all right. There you go. Are you tired? It's going to be all right. Why don't you have a lie down?

EDIE: That'd be nice.

ARTHUR: Shall I help you to bed?

EDIE: Thank you. You'll be all right with him, won't you Stephen? You won't let him fall down or anything.

ARTHUR: You used to say that sort of thing to me about him.

EDIE: Yes, well it's all swings and roundabouts isn't it. Come on.

ARTHUR: There we go.

EDIE: This is the poem of my life. I cannot remember almost everything I have ever done. I cannot remember the names of the children who sat next to me at school. I can hardly tell which of the millions of lives I imagined I might have lived eventually turned out to be the real one. They are all as vivid and vague as each other. Sometimes I cry. It's not even bad yet, sometimes I can't help it. What I remember is light through trees and light on water in the morning and a woman in a white dress and the way the light through my eyelids found me when I used to sunbathe. And your shadow falling over my eyes so I opened them and looked up to see you standing there looking down. My legs in the sun. What I remember is Sundays and walking back from church and my hand in your hand. And you are in all of my dreams because you were there in my life as well.

Exit EDIE and ARTHUR.

STEPHEN looks around. He picks up a box.

End.

WWW.OBERONBOOKS.COM

 Follow us on www.twitter.com/@oberonbooks
& www.facebook.com/oberonbook